MznLnx

Missing Links Exam Preps

Exam Prep for

Brief Applied Calculus

Berresford, Rockett, 3rd Edition

The MznLnx Exam Prep is your link from the texbook and lecture to your exams.
The MznLnx Exam Preps are unauthorized and comprehensive reviews of your textbooks.

All material provided by MznLnx and Rico Publications (c) 2010
Textbook publishers and textbook authors do not particpate in or contribute to these reviews.

MznLnx

Rico Publications

Exam Prep for Brief Applied Calculus
3rd Edition
Berresford, Rockett

Publisher: Raymond Houge
Assistant Editor: Michael Rouger
Text and Cover Designer: Lisa Buckner
Marketing Manager: Sara Swagger
Project Manager, Editorial Production: Jerry Emerson
Art Director: Vernon Lowerui

Product Manager: Dave Mason
Editorial Assitant: Rachel Guzmanji
Pedagogy: Debra Long
Cover Image: Jim Reed/Getty Images
Text and Cover Printer: City Printing, Inc.
Compositor: Media Mix, Inc.

(c) 2010 Rico Publications
ALL RIGHTS RESERVED. No part of this work covered by the copyright may be reproduced or used in any form or by an means--graphic, electronic, or mechanical, including photocopying, recording, taping, Web distribution, information storage, and retrieval systems, or in any other manner--without the written permission of the publisher.

For more information about our products, contact us at:
Dave.Mason@RicoPublications.com

For permission to use material from this text or product, submit a request online to:
Dave.Mason@RicoPublications.com

Printed in the United States
ISBN:

Contents

CHAPTER 1
Functions   1
CHAPTER 2
Derivatives and Their Uses   19
CHAPTER 3
Further Applications of Derivatives   34
CHAPTER 4
Exponential and Logarithmic Functions   49
CHAPTER 5
Integration and Its Applications   63
CHAPTER 6
Integration Techniques and Differential Equations   77
CHAPTER 7
Calculus of Several Variables   92
ANSWER KEY   111

TO THE STUDENT

COMPREHENSIVE

The *MznLnx* Exam Prep series is designed to help you pass your exams. Editors at MznLnx review your textbooks and then prepare these practice exams to help you master the textbook material. Unlike study guides, workbooks, and practice tests provided by the texbook publisher and textbook authors, *MznLnx* gives you **all** of the material in each chapter in exam form, not just samples, so you can be sure to nail your exam.

MECHANICAL

The MznLnx Exam Prep series creates exams that will help you learn the subject matter as well as test you on your understanding. Each question is designed to help you master the concept. Just working through the exams, you gain an understanding of the subject--its a simple mechanical process that produces success.

INTEGRATED STUDY GUIDE AND REVIEW

MznLnx is not just a set of exams designed to test you, its also a comprehensive review of the subject content. Each exam question is also a review of the concept, making sure that you will get the answer correct without having to go to other sources of material. You learn as you go! Its the easiest way to pass an exam.

HUMOR

Studying can be tedious and dry. MznLnx's instructional design includes moderate humor within the exam questions on occassion, to break the tedium and revitalize the brain

Chapter 1. Functions

1. A _____ is a special kind of ratio, indicating a relationship between two measurements with different units, such as miles to gallons or cents to pounds.
   a. Thing
   b. Rate0
   c. Undefined
   d. Undefined

2. _____ is a mathematical subject that includes the study of limits, derivatives, integrals, and power series and constitutes a major part of modern university curriculum.
   a. Thing
   b. Calculus0
   c. Undefined
   d. Undefined

3. _____ systems represent systems whose behavior is not expressible as a sum of the behaviors of its descriptors.
   a. Thing
   b. Nonlinear0
   c. Undefined
   d. Undefined

4. In mathematics, the concept of a _____ tries to capture the intuitive idea of a geometrical one-dimensional and continuous object. A simple example is the circle.
   a. Curve0
   b. Thing
   c. Undefined
   d. Undefined

5. In mathematics, _____ are the intuitive idea of a geometrical one-dimensional and continuous object.
   a. Curves0
   b. Thing
   c. Undefined
   d. Undefined

6. In mathematics, an _____ is a statement about the relative size or order of two objects.
   a. Inequality0
   b. Thing
   c. Undefined
   d. Undefined

7. In mathematics, an inequality is a statement about the relative size or order of two objects. For example 14 > 10, or 14 is _____ 10.
   a. Thing
   b. Greater than0
   c. Undefined
   d. Undefined

8. The _____, the average in everyday English, which is also called the arithmetic _____ (and is distinguished from the geometric _____ or harmonic _____). The average is also called the sample _____. The expected value of a random variable, which is also called the population _____.
   a. Mean0
   b. Thing
   c. Undefined
   d. Undefined

9. In geometry, an _____ is a point at which a line segment or ray terminates.
   a. Endpoint0
   b. Thing
   c. Undefined
   d. Undefined

10. Mathematical _____ is used to represent ideas.
    a. Thing
    b. Notation0
    c. Undefined
    d. Undefined

11. In plane geometry, a _____ is a polygon with four equal sides, four right angles, and parallel opposite sides. In algebra, the _____ of a number is that number multiplied by itself.
   a. Thing
   b. Square0
   c. Undefined
   d. Undefined

12. In mathematics, _____ are used in a variety of notations, including standard notations for intervals, commutators, the Lie bracket, and the Iverson bracket.
   a. Thing
   b. Square Brackets0
   c. Undefined
   d. Undefined

13. In elementary algebra, an _____ is a set that contains every real number between two indicated numbers and may contain the two numbers themselves.
   a. Interval0
   b. Thing
   c. Undefined
   d. Undefined

14. _____ is the notation in which permitted values for a variable are expressed as ranging over a certain interval; "5 < x < 9" is an example of the application of _____.
   a. Thing
   b. Interval notation0
   c. Undefined
   d. Undefined

15. _____, either of the curved-bracket punctuation marks that together make a set of _____
   a. Parentheses0
   b. Thing
   c. Undefined
   d. Undefined

16. In mathematics, _____ geometry was the traditional name for the geometry of three-dimensional Euclidean space — for practical purposes the kind of space we live in.
   a. Thing
   b. Solid0
   c. Undefined
   d. Undefined

17. In mathematics, a _____ may be described informally as a number that can be given by an infinite decimal representation.
   a. Thing
   b. Real number0
   c. Undefined
   d. Undefined

18. _____ are objects, characters, or other concrete representations of ideas, concepts, or other abstractions.
   a. Symbols0
   b. Thing
   c. Undefined
   d. Undefined

19. _____ is the state of being greater than any finite number, however large.
   a. Thing
   b. Infinity0
   c. Undefined
   d. Undefined

20. _____ is the state of being greater than any finite real or natural number, however large.
   a. Thing
   b. Infinite0
   c. Undefined
   d. Undefined

Chapter 1. Functions

21. An _____ is when two lines intersect somewhere on a plane creating a right angle at intersection
    a. Axes0
    b. Thing
    c. Undefined
    d. Undefined

22. In astronomy, geography, geometry and related sciences and contexts, a plane is said to be _____ at a given point if it is locally perpendicular to the gradient of the gravity field, i.e., with the direction of the gravitational force at that point.
    a. Horizontal0
    b. Thing
    c. Undefined
    d. Undefined

23. In mathematics, a _____ is a two-dimensional manifold or surface that is perfectly flat.
    a. Thing
    b. Plane0
    c. Undefined
    d. Undefined

24. _____ means of or relating to the French philosopher and mathematician René Descartes.
    a. Thing
    b. Cartesian0
    c. Undefined
    d. Undefined

25. In geometry, _____ lines are two lines that share one or more common points.
    a. Intersecting0
    b. Thing
    c. Undefined
    d. Undefined

26. An _____ is a straight line around which a geometric figure can be rotated.
    a. Axis0
    b. Thing
    c. Undefined
    d. Undefined

27. An _____ is a collection of two not necessarily distinct objects, one of which is distinguished as the first coordinate and the other as the second coordinate.
    a. Ordered pair0
    b. Thing
    c. Undefined
    d. Undefined

28. The _____ is the y- coordinate of a point within a two dimensional coordinate system. It is sometimes used to refer to the axis rather than the distance along the coordinate system.
    a. Ordinate0
    b. Thing
    c. Undefined
    d. Undefined

29. _____ consists of the first element in a coordinate pair. When graphed in the coordinate plane, it is the distance from the y-axis. Frequently called the x coordinate.
    a. Thing
    b. Abscissa0
    c. Undefined
    d. Undefined

30. _____ was a highly influential French philosopher, mathematician, scientist, and writer. Dubbed the "Founder of Modern Philosophy", and the "Father of Modern Mathematics". His theories provided the basis for the calculus of Newton and Leibniz, by applying infinitesimal calculus to the tangent line problem, thus permitting the evolution of that branch of modern mathematics

a. Descartes0
b. Person
c. Undefined
d. Undefined

31. _____ is often used to describe the measurement of the steepness, incline, gradient, or grade of a straight line. The _____ is defined as the ratio of the "rise" divided by the "run" between two points on a line, or in other words, the ratio of the altitude change to the horizontal distance between any two points on the line.
    a. Slope0
    b. Thing
    c. Undefined
    d. Undefined

32. A _____ is a function that assigns a number to subsets of a given set.
    a. Measure0
    b. Thing
    c. Undefined
    d. Undefined

33. _____, from Latin meaning "to make progress", is defined in two different ways. Pure economic _____ is the increase in wealth that an investor has from making an investment, taking into consideration all costs associated with that investment including the opportunity cost of capital.
    a. Thing
    b. Profit0
    c. Undefined
    d. Undefined

34. A _____ is a symbolic representation denoting a quantity or expression. It often represents an "unknown" quantity that has the potential to change.
    a. Variable0
    b. Thing
    c. Undefined
    d. Undefined

35. A _____ is a set of numbers that designate location in a given reference system, such as x,y in a planar _____ system or an x,y,z in a three-dimensional _____ system.
    a. Coordinate0
    b. Thing
    c. Undefined
    d. Undefined

36. The _____ of measurement are a globally standardized and modernized form of the metric system.
    a. Units0
    b. Thing
    c. Undefined
    d. Undefined

37. The word _____ comes from the Latin word linearis, which means created by lines.
    a. Linear0
    b. Thing
    c. Undefined
    d. Undefined

38. A _____ is an equation in which each term is either a constant or the product of a constant times the first power of a variable.
    a. Thing
    b. Linear equation0
    c. Undefined
    d. Undefined

39. In mathematics and the mathematical sciences, a _____ is a fixed, but possibly unspecified, value. This is in contrast to a variable, which is not fixed.

a. Thing
b. Constant0
c. Undefined
d. Undefined

40. _____ the expected value of a random variable displays the average or central value of the variable. It is a summary value of the distribution of the variable.
   a. Determining0
   b. Thing
   c. Undefined
   d. Undefined

41. In logic and mathematics, _____ is an operation on logical values, for example, the logical value of a proposition, that sends true to false and false to true.
   a. Person
   b. Negation0
   c. Undefined
   d. Undefined

42. A _____ is a negotiable instrument instructing a financial institution to pay a specific amount of a specific currency from a specific demand account held in the maker/depositor's name with that institution. Both the maker and payee may be natural persons or legal entities.
   a. Thing
   b. Check0
   c. Undefined
   d. Undefined

43. A _____ is a statement or claimt that a particular event will occur in the future in more certain terms than a forecast.
   a. Prediction0
   b. Thing
   c. Undefined
   d. Undefined

44. In mathematics, an _____, mean, or central tendency of a data set refers to a measure of the "middle" or "expected" value of the data set.
   a. Average0
   b. Concept
   c. Undefined
   d. Undefined

45. In economics, supply and _____ describe market relations between prospective sellers and buyers of a good.
   a. Thing
   b. Demand0
   c. Undefined
   d. Undefined

46. _____ is the process of reducing the number of significant digits in a number.
   a. Rounding0
   b. Concept
   c. Undefined
   d. Undefined

47. A _____ is a unit of length, usually used to measure distance, in a number of different systems, including Imperial units, United States customary units and Norwegian/Swedish mil. Its size can vary from system to system, but in each is between 1 and 10 kilometers. In contemporary English contexts _____ refers to either:
   a. Thing
   b. Mile0
   c. Undefined
   d. Undefined

48. _____ is a synonym for information.

a. Data0
b. Thing
c. Undefined
d. Undefined

49. _____ is a kind of property which exists as magnitude or multitude. It is among the basic classes of things along with quality, substance, change, and relation.
   a. Amount0
   b. Thing
   c. Undefined
   d. Undefined

50. _____ are economic entities that give rise to future economic benefit and is controlled by the entity as a result of past transaction or other events
   a. Thing
   b. Asset0
   c. Undefined
   d. Undefined

51. _____ is a physical property of a system that underlies the common notions of hot and cold; something that is hotter has the greater _____.
   a. Thing
   b. Temperature0
   c. Undefined
   d. Undefined

52. In Euclidean geometry, a uniform _____ is a linear transformation that enlargers or diminishes objects, and whose _____ factor is the same in all directions. This is also called homothethy.
   a. Scale0
   b. Thing
   c. Undefined
   d. Undefined

53. _____ is, or relates to, the _____ temperature scale .
   a. Thing
   b. Celsius0
   c. Undefined
   d. Undefined

54. _____ is a temperature scale named after the German physicist Daniel Gabriel _____ , who proposed it in 1724.
   a. Thing
   b. Fahrenheit0
   c. Undefined
   d. Undefined

55. In topology and related areas of mathematics a _____ or Moore-Smith sequence is a generalization of a sequence, intended to unify the various notions of limit and generalize them to arbitrary topological spaces.
   a. Thing
   b. Net0
   c. Undefined
   d. Undefined

56. _____ is mass m per unit volume V.
   a. Thing
   b. Density0
   c. Undefined
   d. Undefined

57. _____ is the ability to hold, receive or absorb, or a measure thereof, similar to the concept of volume.
   a. Capacity0
   b. Concept
   c. Undefined
   d. Undefined

Chapter 1. Functions

58. _____ usually refers to the biological _____ of a population level that can be supported for an organism, given the quantity of food, habitat, water and other life infrastructure present.
   a. Thing
   b. Carrying capacity0
   c. Undefined
   d. Undefined

59. Initial objects are also called _____, and terminal objects are also called final.
   a. Thing
   b. Coterminal0
   c. Undefined
   d. Undefined

60. In sociology and biology a _____ is the collection of people or organisms of a particular species living in a given geographic area or space, usually measured by a census.
   a. Thing
   b. Population0
   c. Undefined
   d. Undefined

61. In probability theory and statistics, a _____ is a number dividing the higher half of a sample, a population, or a probability distribution from the lower half.
   a. Concept
   b. Median0
   c. Undefined
   d. Undefined

62. A _____ is a compensation which workers receive in exchange for their labor.
   a. Wage0
   b. Thing
   c. Undefined
   d. Undefined

63. _____ is a way of expressing a number as a fraction of 100 per cent meaning "per hundred".
   a. Percent0
   b. Thing
   c. Undefined
   d. Undefined

64. _____ is the chance that something is likely to happen or be the case.
   a. Probability0
   b. Thing
   c. Undefined
   d. Undefined

65. _____ has many meanings, most of which simply .
   a. Thing
   b. Power0
   c. Undefined
   d. Undefined

66. _____ is a statistical measure of the average length of survival of a living thing.
   a. Life expectancy0
   b. Thing
   c. Undefined
   d. Undefined

67. _____ is a mathematical operation, written a^n, involving two numbers, the base a and the exponent n.
   a. Exponentiating0
   b. Thing
   c. Undefined
   d. Undefined

68. _____ is a mathematical operation, written a^n, involving two numbers, the base a and the exponent n.

a. Thing
c. Undefined
b. Exponentiation0
d. Undefined

69. The mathematical concept of a _____ expresses the intuitive idea of deterministic dependence between two quantities, one of which is viewed as primary and the other as secondary. A _____ then is a way to associate a unique output for each input of a specified type, for example, a real number or an element of a given set.
a. Thing
c. Undefined
b. Function0
d. Undefined

70. In mathematics, a _____ is the result of multiplying, or an expression that identifies factors to be multiplied.
a. Product0
c. Undefined
b. Thing
d. Undefined

71. In mathematics, _____ expressions is used to reduce the expression into the lowest possible term.
a. Simplifying0
c. Undefined
b. Thing
d. Undefined

72. An _____ is a combination of numbers, operators, grouping symbols and/or free variables and bound variables arranged in a meaningful way which can be evaluated..
a. Expression0
c. Undefined
b. Thing
d. Undefined

73. A _____ is the part of a fraction that tells how many equal parts make up a whole, and which is used in the name of the fraction: "halves", "thirds", "fourths" or "quarters", "fifths" and so on.
a. Concept
c. Undefined
b. Denominator0
d. Undefined

74. In linear algebra, the _____ of an n-by-n square matrix A is defined to be the sum of the elements on the main diagonal of A,
a. Trace0
c. Undefined
b. Thing
d. Undefined

75. In mathematics, defined and _____ are used to explain whether or not expressions have meaningful, sensible, and unambiguous values.
a. Thing
c. Undefined
b. Undefined0
d. Undefined

76. In mathematics, the multiplicative inverse of a number x, denoted 1/x or x^{-1}, is the number which, when multiplied by x, yields 1. The multiplicative inverse of x is also called the _____ of x.
a. Thing
c. Undefined
b. Reciprocal0
d. Undefined

77. An _____ of a number a is a number b such that $b^n=a$.
a. Thing
c. Undefined
b. Nth root0
d. Undefined

Chapter 1. Functions

78. _____ is the symbold used to indicate the nth root of a number
    a. Radical0
    b. Thing
    c. Undefined
    d. Undefined

79. In mathematics, a _____ of a number x is a number r such that r^2 = x, or in words, a number r whose square (the result of multiplying the number by itself) is x.
    a. Thing
    b. Square root0
    c. Undefined
    d. Undefined

80. In mathematics, a _____ of a complex-valued function f is a member x of the domain of f such that f(x) vanishes at x, that is, x : f (x) = 0.
    a. Thing
    b. Root0
    c. Undefined
    d. Undefined

81. A _____ is a number that is less than zero.
    a. Thing
    b. Negative number0
    c. Undefined
    d. Undefined

82. A _____ is a three-dimensional solid object bounded by six square faces, facets, or sides, with three meeting at each vertex.
    a. Thing
    b. Cube0
    c. Undefined
    d. Undefined

83. A _____ of a number is a number a such that a^3 = x.
    a. Cube root0
    b. Thing
    c. Undefined
    d. Undefined

84. An _____ is an equality that remains true regardless of the values of any variables that appear within it, to distinguish it from an equality which is true under more particular conditions.
    a. Thing
    b. Identity0
    c. Undefined
    d. Undefined

85. The _____ refers to a relationship between the duration of learning or experience and the resulting progress
    a. Learning curve0
    b. Thing
    c. Undefined
    d. Undefined

86. In mathematics, a _____ is an n-tuple with n being 3.
    a. Triple0
    b. Thing
    c. Undefined
    d. Undefined

87. A _____ of a number is the product of that number with any integer.
    a. Thing
    b. Multiple0
    c. Undefined
    d. Undefined

88. An _____ is the result from the sudden release of stored energy in the Earth's crust that creates seismic waves.

a. Earthquake0
b. Thing
c. Undefined
d. Undefined

89. _____ , was an American seismologist, born in Hamilton, Ohio.
a. Charles Richter0
b. Person
c. Undefined
d. Undefined

90. _____ is an adjective usually refering to being in the centre.
a. Thing
b. Central0
c. Undefined
d. Undefined

91. In mathematics, the _____ of a function is the set of all "output" values produced by that function. Given a function $f : A \to B$, the _____ of f, is defined to be the set $\{x \in B : x = f(a) \text{ for some } a \in A\}$.
a. Thing
b. Range0
c. Undefined
d. Undefined

92. In mathematics, a _____ of a k-place relation $L \subseteq X_1 \times \ldots \times X_k$ is one of the sets X_j, $1 \leq j \leq k$. In the special case where k = 2 and $L \subseteq X_1 \times X_2$ is a function $L : X_1 \to X_2$, it is conventional to refer to X_1 as the _____ of the function and to refer to X_2 as the codomain of the function.
a. Domain0
b. Thing
c. Undefined
d. Undefined

93. In mathematics, an _____ is any of the arguments, i.e. "inputs", to a function. Thus if we have a function f(x), then x is a _____.
a. Thing
b. Independent variable0
c. Undefined
d. Undefined

94. In a function the _____, is the variable which is the value, i.e. the "output", of the function.
a. Dependent variable0
b. Thing
c. Undefined
d. Undefined

95. _____ is a test to determine if a relation or its graph is a function or not
a. Vertical line test0
b. Thing
c. Undefined
d. Undefined

96. In mathematics, the _____ f is the collection of all ordered pairs . In particular, graph means the graphical representation of this collection, in the form of a curve or surface, together with axes, etc. Graphing on a Cartesian plane is sometimes referred to as curve sketching.
a. Graph of a function0
b. Thing
c. Undefined
d. Undefined

97. Acid _____ ratio measures the ability of a company to use its near cash or quick assets to immediately extinguish its current liabilities.
a. Test0
b. Thing
c. Undefined
d. Undefined

Chapter 1. Functions

98. A _____ is a first degree polynomial mathematical function of the form: f(x) = mx + b where m and b are real constants and x is a real variable.
   a. Linear function0
   b. Thing
   c. Undefined
   d. Undefined

99. Fixed costs are expenses whose total does not change in proportion to the activity of a business.Unit fixed costs decline with volume following a retangular hyperbola as the volume of production.Variable costs by contrast change in relation to the activity of a business such as sales or production volume.Along with variable costs,fixed costs make up one of the two components of total cost. In the most simple production function total cost is equal to fixed costs plus variable costs.In accounting terminology, fixed costs will broadly include all costs which are not included in cost of goods sold, and variable costs are those captured in costs of goods sold. The implicit assumption required to make the equivalence between the accounting and economics terminology is that the accounting period is equal to the period in which fixed costs do not vary in relation to production. In practice, this equivalence does not always hold and depending on the period under consideration by management, some overhead expenses can be adjusted by management, and the specific allocation of each expense to each category will be decided under cost accounting.In business planning and management accounting, usage of the terms fixed costs, variable costs and others will often differ from usage in economics, and may depend on the intended use. For example, costs may be segregated into per unit costs fixed costs per period, and variable costs as a proportion of revenue. Capital expenditures will usually be allocated separately, and depending on the purpose, a portion may be regularly allocated to expenses as depreciation and amortization and seen as a _____ per period, or the entire amount may be considered upfront fixed costs.
   a. Thing
   b. Fixed cost0
   c. Undefined
   d. Undefined

100. _____ are expenses whose total does not change in proportion to the activity of a business, within the relevant time period or scale of production
   a. Thing
   b. Fixed costs0
   c. Undefined
   d. Undefined

101. _____ is the change in total cost that arises when the quantity produced changes by one unit.
   a. Marginal cost0
   b. Thing
   c. Undefined
   d. Undefined

102. A _____ is a polynomial function of the form f(x) = ax^2 + bx +c , where a, b, c are real numbers and a , 0.
   a. Quadratic function0
   b. Event
   c. Undefined
   d. Undefined

103. In mathematics, a _____ is a constant multiplicative factor of a certain object. The object can be such things as a variable, a vector, a function, etc. For example, the _____ of 9x^2 is 9.
   a. Coefficient0
   b. Thing
   c. Undefined
   d. Undefined

104. In geometry, the _____ of an object is a point in some sense in the middle of the object.
   a. Center0
   b. Thing
   c. Undefined
   d. Undefined

Chapter 1. Functions

105. In mathematics, the _____ is a conic section generated by the intersection of a right circular conical surface and a plane parallel to a generating straight line of that surface. It can also be defined as locus of points in a plane which are equidistant from a given point.
   a. Parabola0
   b. Thing
   c. Undefined
   d. Undefined

106. In geometry, a _____ is a special kind of point, usually a corner of a polygon, polyhedron, or higher dimensional polytope. In the geometry of curves a _____ is a point of where the first derivative of curvature is zero. In graph theory, a _____ is the fundamental unit out of which graphs are formed
   a. Thing
   b. Vertex0
   c. Undefined
   d. Undefined

107. In mathematics, a _____ is a polynomial equation of the second degree. The general form is $ax^2 + bx + c = 0$.
   a. Thing
   b. Quadratic equation0
   c. Undefined
   d. Undefined

108. In mathematics, _____ is the decomposition of an object into a product of other objects, or factors, which when multiplied together give the original.
   a. Thing
   b. Factoring0
   c. Undefined
   d. Undefined

109. In mathematics, a subset of Euclidean space R^n is called _____ if it is closed and bounded.
   a. Compact0
   b. Thing
   c. Undefined
   d. Undefined

110. _____ is a business term for the amount of money that a company receives from its activities in a given period, mostly from sales of products and/or services to customers
   a. Thing
   b. Revenue0
   c. Undefined
   d. Undefined

111. The plus and _____ signs are mathematical symbols used to represent the notions of positive and negative as well as the operations of addition and subtraction.
   a. Minus0
   b. Thing
   c. Undefined
   d. Undefined

112. _____ are rectangular tables (or grids) of information, often financial information.
   a. Thing
   b. Spreadsheets0
   c. Undefined
   d. Undefined

113. A quadratic equation with real solutions, called roots, which may be real or complex, is given by the _____: $x = \frac{-b \pm \sqrt{b^2 - 4ac}}{2a}$.
   a. Thing
   b. Quadratic formula0
   c. Undefined
   d. Undefined

Chapter 1. Functions

114. _____ of a polynomial with real or complex coefficients is a certain expression in the coefficients of the polynomial which is equal to zero if and only if the polynomial has a multiple root i.e. a root with multiplicity greater than one in the complex numbers.
   a. Discriminant0
   b. Thing
   c. Undefined
   d. Undefined

115. The _____ of a ring R is defined to be the smallest positive integer n such that n a = 0, for all a in R.
   a. Thing
   b. Characteristic0
   c. Undefined
   d. Undefined

116. _____ is a form of periodic payment from an employer to an employee, which is specified in an employment contract.
   a. Thing
   b. Gross pay0
   c. Undefined
   d. Undefined

117. A _____ is a form of periodic payment from an employer to an employee, which is specified in an employment contract.
   a. Thing
   b. Salary0
   c. Undefined
   d. Undefined

118. _____ is the amount of time someone works beyond normal working hours.
   a. Thing
   b. Compensatory time0
   c. Undefined
   d. Undefined

119. _____ is the pressure at some point withig the fluid
   a. Water pressure0
   b. Thing
   c. Undefined
   d. Undefined

120. In geometry, an _____ of a triangle is a straight line through a vertex and perpendicular to (i.e. forming a right angle with) the opposite side or an extension of the opposite side.
   a. Concept
   b. Altitude0
   c. Undefined
   d. Undefined

121. In mathematics, there are several meanings of _____ depending on the subject.
   a. Degree0
   b. Thing
   c. Undefined
   d. Undefined

122. Transport or _____ is the movement of people and goods from one place to another.
   a. Thing
   b. Transportation0
   c. Undefined
   d. Undefined

123. _____ is a unit of speed, expressing the number of international miles covered per hour.
   a. Miles per hour0
   b. Thing
   c. Undefined
   d. Undefined

124. _____ of an object is its speed in a particular direction.

14   *Chapter 1. Functions*

    a. Velocity0   b. Thing
    c. Undefined   d. Undefined

125. _____ are the cyclic rizing and falling of Earth's ocean surface caused by the tidal forces of the Moon and the sun acting on the oceans.
    a. Thing   b. Tides0
    c. Undefined   d. Undefined

126. A _____ is any object propelled through space by the applicationp of a force.
    a. Projectile0   b. Thing
    c. Undefined   d. Undefined

127. _____ is the estimation of a physical quantity such as distance, energy, temperature, or time.
    a. Measurement0   b. Thing
    c. Undefined   d. Undefined

128. _____, in law and economics, is a form of risk management primarily used to hedge against the risk of a contingent loss.
    a. Thing   b. Insurance0
    c. Undefined   d. Undefined

129. In mathematics, a _____ is an expression that is constructed from one or more variables and constants, using only the operations of addition, subtraction, multiplication, and constant positive whole number exponents. is a _____. Note in particular that division by an expression containing a variable is not in general allowed in polynomials. [1]
    a. Thing   b. Polynomial0
    c. Undefined   d. Undefined

130. The _____ is the maximum of the degrees of all terms in the polynomial.
    a. Degree of a polynomial0   b. Thing
    c. Undefined   d. Undefined

131. _____ is the property of a physical object that quantifies the amount of matter and energy it is equivalent to.
    a. Mass0   b. Thing
    c. Undefined   d. Undefined

132. In mathematics, a _____ number is a number which can be expressed as a ratio of two integers. Non-integer _____ numbers (commonly called fractions) are usually written as the vulgar fraction a / b, where b is not zero.
    a. Rational0   b. Thing
    c. Undefined   d. Undefined

133. In mathematics, a _____ is any function which can be written as the ratio of two polynomial functions.
    a. Thing   b. Rational function0
    c. Undefined   d. Undefined

134. In mathematics, _____ growth occurs when the growth rate of a function is always proportional to the function's current size.

Chapter 1. Functions

a. Thing
c. Undefined
b. Exponential0
d. Undefined

135. _____ is one of the most important functions in mathematics. A function commonly used to study growth and decay
a. Exponential function0
c. Undefined
b. Thing
d. Undefined

136. The _____ is the total number of human beings alive on the planet Earth at a given time.
a. Thing
c. Undefined
b. World population0
d. Undefined

137. A _____ defined function $f(x)$ of a real variable x is a function whose definition is given differently on disjoint subsets of its domain.
a. Thing
c. Undefined
b. Piecewise0
d. Undefined

138. A _____ f : $f¶$ ¨ V, where V is a vector space and $f¶$ is a subset of a vector space, is any function with the property that $f¶$ can be decomposed into finitely many convex polytopes, such that f is equal to a linear function on each of these polytopes.
a. Thing
c. Undefined
b. Piecewise linear function0
d. Undefined

139. In Euclidean geometry, a _____ is the set of all points in a plane at a fixed distance, called the radius, from a given point, the center.
a. Thing
c. Undefined
b. Circle0
d. Undefined

140. In mathematics, the _____ (or modulus) of a real number is its numerical value without regard to its sign.
a. Absolute value0
c. Undefined
b. Thing
d. Undefined

141. In mathematics, the _____ of a coordinate system is the point where the axes of the system intersect.
a. Thing
c. Undefined
b. Origin0
d. Undefined

142. In mathematics, a _____ of a positive integer n is a way of writing n as a sum of positive integers.
a. Thing
c. Undefined
b. Composition0
d. Undefined

143. The payment of _____ as remuneration for services rendered or products sold is a common way to reward sales people.
a. Thing
c. Undefined
b. Commission0
d. Undefined

Chapter 1. Functions

144. U.S. liquid _____ is legally defined as 231 cubic inches, and is equal to 3.785411784 litres or abotu 0.13368 cubic feet. This is the most common definition of a _____. The U.S. fluid ounce is defined as 1/128 of a U.S. _____.
    a. Gallon0
    b. Thing
    c. Undefined
    d. Undefined

145. _____ are the basic objects of study in graph theory. Informally speaking, a graph is a set of objects called points, nodes, or vertices connected by links called lines or edges.
    a. Thing
    b. Graphs0
    c. Undefined
    d. Undefined

146. A _____ number is a positive integer which has a positive divisor other than one or itself.
    a. Thing
    b. Composite0
    c. Undefined
    d. Undefined

147. A _____, formed by the composition of one function on another, represents the application of the former to the result of the application of the latter to the argument of the composite.
    a. Thing
    b. Composite function0
    c. Undefined
    d. Undefined

148. In mathematics, a _____ is the end result of a division problem. It can also be expressed as the number of times the divisor divides into the dividend.
    a. Thing
    b. Quotient0
    c. Undefined
    d. Undefined

149. The function difference divided by the point difference is known as the _____
    a. Thing
    b. Difference quotient0
    c. Undefined
    d. Undefined

150. A _____ is a numeral used to indicate a count. The most common use of the word today is to name the part of a fraction that tells the number or count of equal parts.
    a. Thing
    b. Numerator0
    c. Undefined
    d. Undefined

151. Regrouping is the act of putting ones into groups of 10. For example, the 1 on the far right of 131 would be denoted _____ if the digit of the number being subtracted is larger than 1, such as 131-99.
    a. By 100
    b. Thing
    c. Undefined
    d. Undefined

152. In statistics, _____ means the most frequent value assumed by a random variable, or occurring in a sampling of a random variable.
    a. Concept
    b. Mode0
    c. Undefined
    d. Undefined

153. _____ Any process by which a specified characteristic usually amplitude of the output of a device is prevented from exceeding a predetermined value.

Chapter 1. Functions 17

a. Limiting0
c. Undefined
b. Thing
d. Undefined

154. A _____ is a plan of action to guide decisions and actions.
a. Thing
c. Undefined
b. Policy0
d. Undefined

155. _____ is a mathematical notation for describing a set by stating the properties that its members must satisfy.
a. Thing
c. Undefined
b. Set-builder notation0
d. Undefined

156. _____ is a term used in accounting, economics and finance with reference to the fact that assets with finite lives lose value over time.
a. Thing
c. Undefined
b. Depreciation0
d. Undefined

157. _____ is a term applied when talking about the movement of air from one place to the next.
a. Wind speed0
c. Undefined
b. Thing
d. Undefined

158. The population _____ is the total number of human beings alive on the planet Earth at a given time.
a. Thing
c. Undefined
b. Of the world0
d. Undefined

159. A _____ is a type of debt. All material things can be lent but this article focuses exclusively on monetary loans. Like all debt instruments, a _____ entails the redistribution of financial assets over time, between the lender and the borrower.
a. Loan0
c. Undefined
b. Thing
d. Undefined

160. In business, particularly accounting, a _____ is the time intervals that the accounts, statement, payments, or other calculations cover.
a. Thing
c. Undefined
b. Period0
d. Undefined

161. _____ is the fee paid on borrowed money.
a. Interest0
c. Undefined
b. Thing
d. Undefined

162. An _____ is the fee paid on borrow money.
a. Interest rate0
c. Undefined
b. Concept
d. Undefined

163. In functional analysis and related areas of mathematics the _____ set of a given subset of a vector space is a certain set in the dual space.

a. Thing
c. Undefined

b. Polar0
d. Undefined

Chapter 2. Derivatives and Their Uses

1. The _____ is a fundamental concept in analysis. Informally, a function f can be made as close to L as desired, by making x close enough to p.
   a. Limit of a function0
   b. Thing
   c. Undefined
   d. Undefined

2. The mathematical concept of a _____ expresses the intuitive idea of deterministic dependence between two quantities, one of which is viewed as primary and the other as secondary. A _____ then is a way to associate a unique output for each input of a specified type, for example, a real number or an element of a given set.
   a. Function0
   b. Thing
   c. Undefined
   d. Undefined

3. In mathematics, defined and _____ are used to explain whether or not expressions have meaningful, sensible, and unambiguous values.
   a. Undefined0
   b. Thing
   c. Undefined
   d. Undefined

4. In mathematics and the mathematical sciences, a _____ is a fixed, but possibly unspecified, value. This is in contrast to a variable, which is not fixed.
   a. Thing
   b. Constant0
   c. Undefined
   d. Undefined

5. In mathematics, a _____ of a complex-valued function f is a member x of the domain of f such that f(x) vanishes at x, that is, x : f (x) = 0.
   a. Root0
   b. Thing
   c. Undefined
   d. Undefined

6. _____ has many meanings, most of which simply .
   a. Power0
   b. Thing
   c. Undefined
   d. Undefined

7. In mathematics and logic, a _____ proof is a way of showing the truth or falsehood of a given statement by a straightforward combination of established facts, usually existing lemmas and theorems, without making any further assumptions.
   a. Direct0
   b. Thing
   c. Undefined
   d. Undefined

8. In mathematics, _____ expressions is used to reduce the expression into the lowest possible term.
   a. Thing
   b. Simplifying0
   c. Undefined
   d. Undefined

9. In linear algebra, the _____ of an n-by-n square matrix A is defined to be the sum of the elements on the main diagonal of A,
   a. Trace0
   b. Thing
   c. Undefined
   d. Undefined

10. _____ is the study of terms and their use — of words and compound words that are used in specific contexts.

Chapter 2. Derivatives and Their Uses

  a. Thing
  c. Undefined
  b. Terminology0
  d. Undefined

11. The _____, the average in everyday English, which is also called the arithmetic _____ (and is distinguished from the geometric _____ or harmonic _____). The average is also called the sample _____. The expected value of a random variable, which is also called the population _____.
  a. Mean0
  c. Undefined
  b. Thing
  d. Undefined

12. An _____ is a combination of numbers, operators, grouping symbols and/or free variables and bound variables arranged in a meaningful way which can be evaluated..
  a. Thing
  c. Undefined
  b. Expression0
  d. Undefined

13. _____ is a straight line or curve A to which another curve B the one being studied approaches closer and closer as one moves along it.
  a. Vertical asymptote0
  c. Undefined
  b. Thing
  d. Undefined

14. _____ are the basic objects of study in graph theory. Informally speaking, a graph is a set of objects called points, nodes, or vertices connected by links called lines or edges.
  a. Thing
  c. Undefined
  b. Graphs0
  d. Undefined

15. An _____ is a straight line or curve A to which another curve B approaches closer and closer as one moves along it. As one moves along B, the space between it and the _____ A becomes smaller and smaller, and can in fact be made as small as one could wish by going far enough along. A curve may or may not touch or cross its _____. In fact, the curve may intersect the _____ an infinite number of times.
  a. Thing
  c. Undefined
  b. Asymptote0
  d. Undefined

16. Mathematical _____ is used to represent ideas.
  a. Thing
  c. Undefined
  b. Notation0
  d. Undefined

17. In common philosophical language, a proposition or _____, is the content of an assertion, that is, it is true-or-false and defined by the meaning of a particular piece of language.
  a. Concept
  c. Undefined
  b. Statement0
  d. Undefined

18. A _____ is a symbolic representation denoting a quantity or expression. It often represents an "unknown" quantity that has the potential to change.
  a. Variable0
  c. Undefined
  b. Thing
  d. Undefined

Chapter 2. Derivatives and Their Uses

19. A _____ function is a function for which, intuitively, small changes in the input result in small changes in the output.
   a. Continuous0
   b. Event
   c. Undefined
   d. Undefined

20. In geometry, an _____ is a point at which a line segment or ray terminates.
   a. Endpoint0
   b. Thing
   c. Undefined
   d. Undefined

21. In elementary algebra, an _____ is a set that contains every real number between two indicated numbers and may contain the two numbers themselves.
   a. Thing
   b. Interval0
   c. Undefined
   d. Undefined

22. A _____ is a polynomial function of the form f(x) = ax^2 + bx +c , where a, b, c are real numbers and a , 0.
   a. Quadratic function0
   b. Event
   c. Undefined
   d. Undefined

23. In mathematics, the _____ is a conic section generated by the intersection of a right circular conical surface and a plane parallel to a generating straight line of that surface. It can also be defined as locus of points in a plane which are equidistant from a given point.
   a. Parabola0
   b. Thing
   c. Undefined
   d. Undefined

24. The word _____ comes from the Latin word linearis, which means created by lines.
   a. Linear0
   b. Thing
   c. Undefined
   d. Undefined

25. In mathematics, a _____ number is a number which can be expressed as a ratio of two integers. Non-integer _____ numbers (commonly called fractions) are usually written as the vulgar fraction a / b, where b is not zero.
   a. Rational0
   b. Thing
   c. Undefined
   d. Undefined

26. In mathematics, a _____ is any function which can be written as the ratio of two polynomial functions.
   a. Rational function0
   b. Thing
   c. Undefined
   d. Undefined

27. A _____ is the part of a fraction that tells how many equal parts make up a whole, and which is used in the name of the fraction: "halves", "thirds", "fourths" or "quarters", "fifths" and so on.
   a. Concept
   b. Denominator0
   c. Undefined
   d. Undefined

28. _____ the expected value of a random variable displays the average or central value of the variable.It is a summary value of the distribution of the variable.

a. Determining0
b. Thing
c. Undefined
d. Undefined

29. In mathematics, _____ growth occurs when the growth rate of a function is always proportional to the function's current size.
   a. Thing
   b. Exponential0
   c. Undefined
   d. Undefined

30. _____ is one of the most important functions in mathematics. A function commonly used to study growth and decay
   a. Thing
   b. Exponential function0
   c. Undefined
   d. Undefined

31. In mathematics, a _____ is an expression that is constructed from one or more variables and constants, using only the operations of addition, subtraction, multiplication, and constant positive whole number exponents. is a _____. Note in particular that division by an expression containing a variable is not in general allowed in polynomials. [1]
   a. Thing
   b. Polynomial0
   c. Undefined
   d. Undefined

32. In mathematics, _____ is an elementary arithmetic operation. When one of the numbers is a whole number, _____ is the repeated sum of the other number.
   a. Multiplication0
   b. Thing
   c. Undefined
   d. Undefined

33. A _____ is a first degree polynomial mathematical function of the form: $f(x) = mx + b$ where m and b are real constants and x is a real variable.
   a. Thing
   b. Linear function0
   c. Undefined
   d. Undefined

34. A _____ defined function $f(x)$ of a real variable x is a function whose definition is given differently on disjoint subsets of its domain.
   a. Piecewise0
   b. Thing
   c. Undefined
   d. Undefined

35. A _____ $f : f¶ \to V$, where V is a vector space and $f¶$ is a subset of a vector space, is any function with the property that $f¶$ can be decomposed into finitely many convex polytopes, such that f is equal to a linear function on each of these polytopes.
   a. Piecewise linear function0
   b. Thing
   c. Undefined
   d. Undefined

36. _____ of an object is its speed in a particular direction.
   a. Thing
   b. Velocity0
   c. Undefined
   d. Undefined

37. The _____ in a vacuum is an important physical constant denoted by the letter c for constant or the Latin word celeritas meaning "swiftness

Chapter 2. Derivatives and Their Uses

a. Speed of light0   b. Thing
c. Undefined   d. Undefined

38. _____ is electromagnetic radiation with a wavelength that is visible to the eye (visible _____) or, in a technical or scientific context, electromagnetic radiation of any wavelength.
   a. Light0   b. Thing
   c. Undefined   d. Undefined

39. A _____ is a special kind of ratio, indicating a relationship between two measurements with different units, such as miles to gallons or cents to pounds.
   a. Thing   b. Rate0
   c. Undefined   d. Undefined

40. In mathematics, an _____, mean, or central tendency of a data set refers to a measure of the "middle" or "expected" value of the data set.
   a. Average0   b. Concept
   c. Undefined   d. Undefined

41. _____ is a physical property of a system that underlies the common notions of hot and cold; something that is hotter has the greater _____.
   a. Temperature0   b. Thing
   c. Undefined   d. Undefined

42. The _____ of measurement are a globally standardized and modernized form of the metric system.
   a. Thing   b. Units0
   c. Undefined   d. Undefined

43. _____ of a curve is a line that intersects two or more points on the curve.
   a. Secant line0   b. Thing
   c. Undefined   d. Undefined

44. In mathematics, the concept of a _____ tries to capture the intuitive idea of a geometrical one-dimensional and continuous object. A simple example is the circle.
   a. Thing   b. Curve0
   c. Undefined   d. Undefined

45. _____ is a trigonometric function that is the reciprocal of cosine.
   a. Secant0   b. Thing
   c. Undefined   d. Undefined

46. In trigonometry, the _____ is a function defined as $\tan x = \sin x / \cos x$. The function is so-named because it can be defined as the length of a certain segment of a _____ (in the geometric sense) to the unit circle. In plane geometry, a line is _____ to a curve, at some point, if both line and curve pass through the point with the same direction.
   a. Tangent0   b. Thing
   c. Undefined   d. Undefined

Chapter 2. Derivatives and Their Uses

47. _____ has two distinct but etymologically-related meanings: one in geometry and one in trigonometry.
    a. Tangent line0
    b. Thing
    c. Undefined
    d. Undefined

48. _____ is often used to describe the measurement of the steepness, incline, gradient, or grade of a straight line. The _____ is defined as the ratio of the "rise" divided by the "run" between two points on a line, or in other words, the ratio of the altitude change to the horizontal distance between any two points on the line.
    a. Thing
    b. Slope0
    c. Undefined
    d. Undefined

49. In mathematics, a _____ is the end result of a division problem. It can also be expressed as the number of times the divisor divides into the dividend.
    a. Quotient0
    b. Thing
    c. Undefined
    d. Undefined

50. The _____ is a measurement of how a function changes when the values of its inputs change.
    a. Derivative0
    b. Thing
    c. Undefined
    d. Undefined

51. In physics, _____ is an influence that may cause an object to accelerate. It may be experienced as a lift, a push, or a pull. The actual acceleration of the body is determined by the vector sum of all forces acting on it, known as net _____ or resultant _____.
    a. Force0
    b. Thing
    c. Undefined
    d. Undefined

52. A _____ is a simplified and structured visual representation of concepts, ideas, constructions, relations, statistical data, anatomy etc used in all aspects of human activities to visualize and clarify the topic.
    a. Diagram0
    b. Thing
    c. Undefined
    d. Undefined

53. A _____ is a deliberate process for transforming one or more inputs into one or more results.
    a. Thing
    b. Calculation0
    c. Undefined
    d. Undefined

54. The function difference divided by the point difference is known as the _____
    a. Thing
    b. Difference quotient0
    c. Undefined
    d. Undefined

55. _____, a field in mathematics, is the study of how functions change when their inputs change. The primary object of study in _____ is the derivative.
    a. Differential calculus0
    b. Thing
    c. Undefined
    d. Undefined

56. In mathematics, a _____ is the result of multiplying, or an expression that identifies factors to be multiplied.

Chapter 2. Derivatives and Their Uses

    a. Product0   b. Thing
    c. Undefined   d. Undefined

57. In mathematics, there are several meanings of _____ depending on the subject.
    a. Thing   b. Degree0
    c. Undefined   d. Undefined

58. Sir Isaac _____, was an English physicist, mathematician, astronomer, natural philosopher, and alchemist, regarded by many as the greatest figure in the history of science
    a. Newton0   b. Person
    c. Undefined   d. Undefined

59. _____ was a German mathematician and philosopher. He invented calculus independently of Newton, and his notation is the one in general use since.
    a. Leibniz0   b. Person
    c. Undefined   d. Undefined

60. _____ is a mathematical subject that includes the study of limits, derivatives, integrals, and power series and constitutes a major part of modern university curriculum.
    a. Calculus0   b. Thing
    c. Undefined   d. Undefined

61. Sir _____ was an English physicist, mathematician, astronomer, natural philosopher, and alchemist, regarded by many as the greatest figure in the history of science.
    a. Person   b. Isaac Newton0
    c. Undefined   d. Undefined

62. In mathematics, a _____ number (or a _____) is a natural number that has exactly two (distinct) natural number divisors, which are 1 and the _____ number itself.
    a. Thing   b. Prime0
    c. Undefined   d. Undefined

63. In business, particularly accounting, a _____ is the time intervals that the accounts, statement, payments, or other calculations cover.
    a. Thing   b. Period0
    c. Undefined   d. Undefined

64. _____ is the transport of people on a trip/journey or the process or time involved in a person or object moving from one location to another.
    a. Travel0   b. Thing
    c. Undefined   d. Undefined

65. A _____ is a unit of length, usually used to measure distance, in a number of different systems, including Imperial units, United States customary units and Norwegian/Swedish mil. Its size can vary from system to system, but in each is between 1 and 10 kilometers. In contemporary English contexts _____ refers to either:

a. Mile0
b. Thing
c. Undefined
d. Undefined

66. In mathematics, an _____ is any of the arguments, i.e. "inputs", to a function. Thus if we have a function f(x), then x is a _____.
   a. Independent variable0
   b. Thing
   c. Undefined
   d. Undefined

67. A _____ is a numeral used to indicate a count. The most common use of the word today is to name the part of a fraction that tells the number or count of equal parts.
   a. Thing
   b. Numerator0
   c. Undefined
   d. Undefined

68. _____ are a measure of time.
   a. Thing
   b. Minutes0
   c. Undefined
   d. Undefined

69. In sociology and biology a _____ is the collection of people or organisms of a particular species living in a given geographic area or space, usually measured by a census.
   a. Thing
   b. Population0
   c. Undefined
   d. Undefined

70. In the scientific method, an _____ (Latin: ex-+-periri, "of (or from) trying"), is a set of actions and observations, performed in the context of solving a particular problem or question, in order to support or falsify a hypothesis or research concerning phenomena.
   a. Experiment0
   b. Thing
   c. Undefined
   d. Undefined

71. _____ is a temperature scale named after the German physicist Daniel Gabriel _____ , who proposed it in 1724.
   a. Thing
   b. Fahrenheit0
   c. Undefined
   d. Undefined

72. _____ is a function whose values do not vary and thus are constant.
   a. Constant function0
   b. Thing
   c. Undefined
   d. Undefined

73. In astronomy, geography, geometry and related sciences and contexts, a plane is said to be _____ at a given point if it is locally perpendicular to the gradient of the gravity field, i.e., with the direction of the gravitational force at that point.
   a. Horizontal0
   b. Thing
   c. Undefined
   d. Undefined

74. A _____ is the result of the addition of a set of numbers. The numbers may be natural numbers, complex numbers, matrices, or still more complicated objects. An infinite _____ is a subtle procedure known as a series.

Chapter 2. Derivatives and Their Uses

a. Thing
b. Sum0
c. Undefined
d. Undefined

75. In calculus, the _____ in differentiation is a method of finding the derivative of a function that is the sum of two other functions for which derivatives exist.
   a. Sum Rule0
   b. Thing
   c. Undefined
   d. Undefined

76. _____, from Latin meaning "to make progress", is defined in two different ways. Pure economic _____ is the increase in wealth that an investor has from making an investment, taking into consideration all costs associated with that investment including the opportunity cost of capital.
   a. Profit0
   b. Thing
   c. Undefined
   d. Undefined

77. _____ is the extra revenue that an additional unit of product will bring a firm. It can also be described as the change in total revenue/change in number of units sold.
   a. Thing
   b. Marginal revenue0
   c. Undefined
   d. Undefined

78. _____ is a business term for the amount of money that a company receives from its activities in a given period, mostly from sales of products and/or services to customers
   a. Thing
   b. Revenue0
   c. Undefined
   d. Undefined

79. _____ is the application of tools and a processing medium to the transformation of raw materials into finished goods for sale.
   a. Thing
   b. Manufacturing0
   c. Undefined
   d. Undefined

80. _____ is the change in total cost that arises when the quantity produced changes by one unit.
   a. Marginal cost0
   b. Thing
   c. Undefined
   d. Undefined

81. _____ is the fee paid on borrowed money.
   a. Interest0
   b. Thing
   c. Undefined
   d. Undefined

82. A _____ of a number is the product of that number with any integer.
   a. Multiple0
   b. Thing
   c. Undefined
   d. Undefined

83. _____ is a method for differentiating expressions involving exponentiation the power operation.
   a. Power rule0
   b. Thing
   c. Undefined
   d. Undefined

Chapter 2. Derivatives and Their Uses

84. In epidemiology, an _____ is a disease that appears as new cases in a given human population, during a given period, at a rate that substantially exceeds with is "expected," based on recent experience.
    a. Epidemic0
    b. Thing
    c. Undefined
    d. Undefined

85. _____ is a kind of property which exists as magnitude or multitude. It is among the basic classes of things along with quality, substance, change, and relation.
    a. Thing
    b. Amount0
    c. Undefined
    d. Undefined

86. _____ is the flow of blood in the cardiovascular system.
    a. Blood flow0
    b. Thing
    c. Undefined
    d. Undefined

87. _____ is the level of functional and/or metabolic efficiency of an organism at both the micro level.
    a. Health0
    b. Thing
    c. Undefined
    d. Undefined

88. A _____ is a function that assigns a number to subsets of a given set.
    a. Measure0
    b. Thing
    c. Undefined
    d. Undefined

89. _____ is the chance that something is likely to happen or be the case.
    a. Thing
    b. Probability0
    c. Undefined
    d. Undefined

90. _____ is a way of expressing a number as a fraction of 100 per cent meaning "per hundred".
    a. Thing
    b. Percent0
    c. Undefined
    d. Undefined

91. _____ is a synonym for information.
    a. Thing
    b. Data0
    c. Undefined
    d. Undefined

92. A _____ fraction is a fraction in which the absolute value of the numerator is less than the denominator--hence, the absolute value of the fraction is less than 1.
    a. Thing
    b. Proper0
    c. Undefined
    d. Undefined

93. The _____ governs the differentiation of products of differentiable functions.
    a. Thing
    b. Product rule0
    c. Undefined
    d. Undefined

94. A _____ is a negotiable instrument instructing a financial institution to pay a specific amount of a specific currency from a specific demand account held in the maker/depositor's name with that institution. Both the maker and payee may be natural persons or legal entities.

Chapter 2. Derivatives and Their Uses

    a. Check0   b. Thing
    c. Undefined   d. Undefined

95. The _____ is a method of finding the derivative of a function that is the quotient of two other functions for which derivatives exist.
    a. Thing   b. Quotient rule0
    c. Undefined   d. Undefined

96. U.S. liquid _____ is legally defined as 231 cubic inches, and is equal to 3.785411784 litres or abotu 0.13368 cubic feet. This is the most common definition of a _____. The U.S. fluid ounce is defined as 1/128 of a U.S. _____.
    a. Thing   b. Gallon0
    c. Undefined   d. Undefined

97. _____ is the property of a physical object that quantifies the amount of matter and energy it is equivalent to.
    a. Mass0   b. Thing
    c. Undefined   d. Undefined

98. _____, in economics and political economy, are the distributions or payments awarded to the various suppliers of the factors of production.
    a. Returns0   b. Thing
    c. Undefined   d. Undefined

99. According to _____ relationship, in a production system with fixed and variable inputs , beyond some point, each additional unit of variable input yields less and less additional output.
    a. Thing   b. Diminishing returns0
    c. Undefined   d. Undefined

100. _____ is a unit of speed, expressing the number of international miles covered per hour.
    a. Thing   b. Miles per hour0
    c. Undefined   d. Undefined

101. _____ is a mathematical operation, written a^n, involving two numbers, the base a and the exponent n.
    a. Exponentiating0   b. Thing
    c. Undefined   d. Undefined

102. _____ is a mathematical operation, written a^n, involving two numbers, the base a and the exponent n.
    a. Thing   b. Exponentiation0
    c. Undefined   d. Undefined

103. In topology and related areas of mathematics a _____ or Moore-Smith sequence is a generalization of a sequence, intended to unify the various notions of limit and generalize them to arbitrary topological spaces.
    a. Net0   b. Thing
    c. Undefined   d. Undefined

104. _____ is mass m per unit volume V.

Chapter 2. Derivatives and Their Uses

a. Density0
b. Thing
c. Undefined
d. Undefined

105. In geographic information systems, a _____ comprises an entity with a geographic location, typically determined by points, arcs, or polygons. Carriageways and cadastres exemplify _____ data.
a. Feature0
b. Thing
c. Undefined
d. Undefined

106. An _____ is a term used to describe an allocation of money from one person to another.
a. Thing
b. Allowance0
c. Undefined
d. Undefined

107. _____, either of the curved-bracket punctuation marks that together make a set of _____
a. Thing
b. Parentheses0
c. Undefined
d. Undefined

108. _____ is defined as the rate of change or derivative with respect to time of velocity.
a. Thing
b. Acceleration0
c. Undefined
d. Undefined

109. In physics, _____ is the rate of change of acceleration; more precisely, the derivative of acceleration with respect to time, the second derivative of velocity, or the third derivative of displacement. _____ is described by the following equation:
a. Jerk0
b. Thing
c. Undefined
d. Undefined

110. _____, Greek for "knowledge of nature," is the branch of science concerned with the discovery and characterization of universal laws which govern matter, energy, space, and time.
a. Thing
b. Physics0
c. Undefined
d. Undefined

111. _____ is change in population over time, and can be quantified as the change in the number of individuals in a population per unit time.
a. Thing
b. Population growth0
c. Undefined
d. Undefined

112. A _____ is an individual or household that purchases and uses goods and services generated within the economy.
a. Thing
b. Consumer0
c. Undefined
d. Undefined

113. In mathematics, a _____ or rhodonea curve is a sinusoid plotted in polar coordinates.
a. Rose0
b. Thing
c. Undefined
d. Undefined

Chapter 2. Derivatives and Their Uses

114. _____ is dedicated to the interests of mathematical research and scholarship, which it does with various publications and conferences as well as annual monetary awards to mathematicians.
    a. American Mathematical Society0
    b. Thing
    c. Undefined
    d. Undefined

115. A _____ is 360° or 2ð radians.
    a. Thing
    b. Turn0
    c. Undefined
    d. Undefined

116. In functional analysis and related areas of mathematics the _____ set of a given subset of a vector space is a certain set in the dual space.
    a. Thing
    b. Polar0
    c. Undefined
    d. Undefined

117. _____ is a term applied when talking about the movement of air from one place to the next.
    a. Thing
    b. Wind speed0
    c. Undefined
    d. Undefined

118. The word _____ is used in a variety of ways in mathematics.
    a. Thing
    b. Index0
    c. Undefined
    d. Undefined

119. In calculus, the _____ is a formula for the derivative of the composite of two functions.
    a. Chain rule0
    b. Concept
    c. Undefined
    d. Undefined

120. In mathematics, a _____ of a positive integer n is a way of writing n as a sum of positive integers.
    a. Thing
    b. Composition0
    c. Undefined
    d. Undefined

121. A _____ number is a positive integer which has a positive divisor other than one or itself.
    a. Composite0
    b. Thing
    c. Undefined
    d. Undefined

122. A _____, formed by the composition of one function on another, represents the application of the former to the result of the application of the latter to the argument of the composite.
    a. Composite function0
    b. Thing
    c. Undefined
    d. Undefined

123. In classical geometry, a _____ of a circle or sphere is any line segment from its center to its boundary. By extension, the _____ of a circle or sphere is the length of any such segment. The _____ is half the diameter. In science and engineering the term _____ of curvature is commonly used as a synonym for _____.
    a. Radius0
    b. Thing
    c. Undefined
    d. Undefined

Chapter 2. Derivatives and Their Uses

124. In mathematics, a _____ can mean either an element of the set {1, 2, 3, ...} (i.e the positive integers) or an element of the set {0, 1, 2, 3, ...} (i.e. the non-negative integers).
    a. Whole number0
    b. Concept
    c. Undefined
    d. Undefined

125. In Euclidean geometry, a uniform _____ is a linear transformation that enlargers or diminishes objects, and whose _____ factor is the same in all directions. This is also called homothethy.
    a. Scale0
    b. Thing
    c. Undefined
    d. Undefined

126. In mathematics, factorization (British English: factorisation) or factoring is the decomposition of an object (for example, a number, a polynomial, or a matrix) into a product of other objects, or _____, which when multiplied together give the original.
    a. Thing
    b. Factors0
    c. Undefined
    d. Undefined

127. In mathematics, the _____ of a coordinate system is the point where the axes of the system intersect.
    a. Thing
    b. Origin0
    c. Undefined
    d. Undefined

128. In mathematics, the _____ (or modulus) of a real number is its numerical value without regard to its sign.
    a. Thing
    b. Absolute value0
    c. Undefined
    d. Undefined

129. _____ are rectangular tables (or grids) of information, often financial information.
    a. Spreadsheets0
    b. Thing
    c. Undefined
    d. Undefined

130. In mathematics, a matrix can be thought of as each row or _____ being a vector. Hence, a space formed by row vectors or _____ vectors are said to be a row space or a _____ space.
    a. Column0
    b. Concept
    c. Undefined
    d. Undefined

131. The _____ refers to a relationship between the duration of learning or experience and the resulting progress
    a. Thing
    b. Learning curve0
    c. Undefined
    d. Undefined

132. The _____ of a solid object is the three-dimensional concept of how much space it occupies, often quantified numerically.
    a. Thing
    b. Volume0
    c. Undefined
    d. Undefined

133. A _____ is any object propelled through space by the applicationp of a force.
    a. Projectile0
    b. Thing
    c. Undefined
    d. Undefined

Chapter 2. Derivatives and Their Uses

134. Continuous functions are of utmost importance in mathematics and applications. However, not all functions are continuous. If a function is not continuous at a point in its domain, one says that it has a _____ there. The set of all points of _____ of a function may be a discrete set, a dense set, or even the entire domain of the function.
   a. Discontinuity0
   b. Thing
   c. Undefined
   d. Undefined

135. In mathematics, _____ are the intuitive idea of a geometrical one-dimensional and continuous object.
   a. Curves0
   b. Thing
   c. Undefined
   d. Undefined

136. In mathematics, a _____ is a two-dimensional manifold or surface that is perfectly flat.
   a. Plane0
   b. Thing
   c. Undefined
   d. Undefined

137. In Euclidean geometry, a _____ is the set of all points in a plane at a fixed distance, called the radius, from a given point, the center.
   a. Thing
   b. Circle0
   c. Undefined
   d. Undefined

138. The _____ is the distance around a closed curve. _____ is a kind of perimeter.
   a. Thing
   b. Circumference0
   c. Undefined
   d. Undefined

139. In mathematics, a _____ is the set of all points in three-dimensional space (R^3) which are at distance r from a fixed point of that space, where r is a positive real number called the radius of the _____. The fixed point is called the center or centre, and is not part of the _____ itself.
   a. Sphere0
   b. Thing
   c. Undefined
   d. Undefined

140. A _____ is a vehicle, missile or aircraft which obtains thrust by the reaction to the ejection of fast moving fluid from within a _____ engine.
   a. Thing
   b. Rocket0
   c. Undefined
   d. Undefined

141. _____ interest refers to the fact that whenever interest is calculated, it is based not only on the original principal, but also on any unpaid interest that has been added to the principal.
   a. Thing
   b. Compound0
   c. Undefined
   d. Undefined

142. _____ refers to the fact that whenever interest is calculated, it is based not only on the original principal, but also on any unpaid interest that has been added to the principal. The more frequently interest is compounded, the faster the balance grows.
   a. Compound interest0
   b. Concept
   c. Undefined
   d. Undefined

Chapter 3. Further Applications of Derivatives

1. In mathematics, the concept of a _____ tries to capture the intuitive idea of a geometrical one-dimensional and continuous object. A simple example is the circle.
   a. Curve0
   b. Thing
   c. Undefined
   d. Undefined

2. _____ is a mathematical subject that includes the study of limits, derivatives, integrals, and power series and constitutes a major part of modern university curriculum.
   a. Thing
   b. Calculus0
   c. Undefined
   d. Undefined

3. In elementary algebra, an _____ is a set that contains every real number between two indicated numbers and may contain the two numbers themselves.
   a. Interval0
   b. Thing
   c. Undefined
   d. Undefined

4. An _____ or an extremal point is a point that belongs to the extremity of something.
   a. Thing
   b. Extreme point0
   c. Undefined
   d. Undefined

5. The _____ is the highest point in a certain portion of a graph.
   a. Relative maximum0
   b. Thing
   c. Undefined
   d. Undefined

6. The _____, the average in everyday English, which is also called the arithmetic _____ (and is distinguished from the geometric _____ or harmonic _____). The average is also called the sample _____. The expected value of a random variable, which is also called the population _____.
   a. Mean0
   b. Thing
   c. Undefined
   d. Undefined

7. The _____ is a measurement of how a function changes when the values of its inputs change.
   a. Thing
   b. Derivative0
   c. Undefined
   d. Undefined

8. In mathematics, defined and _____ are used to explain whether or not expressions have meaningful, sensible, and unambiguous values.
   a. Thing
   b. Undefined0
   c. Undefined
   d. Undefined

9. _____ are the basic objects of study in graph theory. Informally speaking, a graph is a set of objects called points, nodes, or vertices connected by links called lines or edges.
   a. Graphs0
   b. Thing
   c. Undefined
   d. Undefined

10. _____ is often used to describe the measurement of the steepness, incline, gradient, or grade of a straight line. The _____ is defined as the ratio of the "rise" divided by the "run" between two points on a line, or in other words, the ratio of the altitude change to the horizontal distance between any two points on the line.

Chapter 3. Further Applications of Derivatives

a. Thing
b. Slope0
c. Undefined
d. Undefined

11. In trigonometry, the _____ is a function defined as tan x = $^{sin\ x}/_{cos\ x}$. The function is so-named because it can be defined as the length of a certain segment of a _____ (in the geometric sense) to the unit circle. In plane geometry, a line is _____ to a curve, at some point, if both line and curve pass through the point with the same direction.
a. Thing
b. Tangent0
c. Undefined
d. Undefined

12. In astronomy, geography, geometry and related sciences and contexts, a plane is said to be _____ at a given point if it is locally perpendicular to the gradient of the gravity field, i.e., with the direction of the gravitational force at that point.
a. Horizontal0
b. Thing
c. Undefined
d. Undefined

13. _____ has two distinct but etymologically-related meanings: one in geometry and one in trigonometry.
a. Thing
b. Tangent line0
c. Undefined
d. Undefined

14. The mathematical concept of a _____ expresses the intuitive idea of deterministic dependence between two quantities, one of which is viewed as primary and the other as secondary. A _____ then is a way to associate a unique output for each input of a specified type, for example, a real number or an element of a given set.
a. Thing
b. Function0
c. Undefined
d. Undefined

15. In mathematics, a _____ of a k-place relation L ⊆ X_1 × ... × X_k is one of the sets X_j, 1 ≤ j ≤ k. In the special case where k = 2 and L ⊆ X_1 × X_2 is a function L : X_1 → X_2, it is conventional to refer to X_1 as the _____ of the function and to refer to X_2 as the codomain of the function.
a. Domain0
b. Thing
c. Undefined
d. Undefined

16. A _____ function is a function for which, intuitively, small changes in the input result in small changes in the output.
a. Continuous0
b. Event
c. Undefined
d. Undefined

17. _____ means in succession or back-to-back
a. Thing
b. Consecutive0
c. Undefined
d. Undefined

18. Acid _____ ratio measures the ability of a company to use its near cash or quick assets to immediately extinguish its current liabilities.
a. Thing
b. Test0
c. Undefined
d. Undefined

19. A _____ is a simplified and structured visual representation of concepts, ideas, constructions, relations, statistical data, anatomy etc used in all aspects of human activities to visualize and clarify the topic.

Chapter 3. Further Applications of Derivatives

  a. Thing
  c. Undefined
  b. Diagram0
  d. Undefined

20. The _____ is the lowest point in a certain portion of a graph.
  a. Thing
  c. Undefined
  b. Relative minimum0
  d. Undefined

21. A _____ is a negotiable instrument instructing a financial institution to pay a specific amount of a specific currency from a specific demand account held in the maker/depositor's name with that institution. Both the maker and payee may be natural persons or legal entities.
  a. Check0
  c. Undefined
  b. Thing
  d. Undefined

22. In mathematics, _____ is the decomposition of an object into a product of other objects, or factors, which when multiplied together give the original.
  a. Factoring0
  c. Undefined
  b. Thing
  d. Undefined

23. In mathematics, a _____ number is a number which can be expressed as a ratio of two integers. Non-integer _____ numbers (commonly called fractions) are usually written as the vulgar fraction a / b, where b is not zero.
  a. Thing
  c. Undefined
  b. Rational0
  d. Undefined

24. In mathematics, a _____ is any function which can be written as the ratio of two polynomial functions.
  a. Thing
  c. Undefined
  b. Rational function0
  d. Undefined

25. _____ is the fee paid on borrowed money.
  a. Interest0
  c. Undefined
  b. Thing
  d. Undefined

26. In mathematics, the _____, sometimes called the witch of Maria Agnesi is the curve defined as follows. Starting with a fixed circle, a point O on the circle is chosen. For any other point A on the circle, the secant line OA is drawn. The point M is diametrically opposite O. The line OA intersects the tangent at M at the point N. The line parallel to OM through N, and the line perpendicular to OM through A intersect at P. As the point A is varied, the path of P is the witch.
  a. Witch of Agnesi0
  c. Undefined
  b. Thing
  d. Undefined

27. In geometry, a _____ is a special kind of point, usually a corner of a polygon, polyhedron, or higher dimensional polytope. In the geometry of curves a _____ is a point of where the first derivative of curvature is zero. In graph theory, a _____ is the fundamental unit out of which graphs are formed
  a. Thing
  c. Undefined
  b. Vertex0
  d. Undefined

28. In mathematics, the _____ is a conic section generated by the intersection of a right circular conical surface and a plane parallel to a generating straight line of that surface. It can also be defined as locus of points in a plane which are equidistant from a given point.
   a. Parabola0
   b. Thing
   c. Undefined
   d. Undefined

29. A _____ is a set of numbers that designate location in a given reference system, such as x,y in a planar _____ system or an x,y,z in a three-dimensional _____ system.
   a. Thing
   b. Coordinate0
   c. Undefined
   d. Undefined

30. In sociology and biology a _____ is the collection of people or organisms of a particular species living in a given geographic area or space, usually measured by a census.
   a. Population0
   b. Thing
   c. Undefined
   d. Undefined

31. In mathematics, _____ are the intuitive idea of a geometrical one-dimensional and continuous object.
   a. Thing
   b. Curves0
   c. Undefined
   d. Undefined

32. The _____ refers to a relationship between the duration of learning or experience and the resulting progress
   a. Thing
   b. Learning curve0
   c. Undefined
   d. Undefined

33. _____ is a kind of property which exists as magnitude or multitude. It is among the basic classes of things along with quality, substance, change, and relation.
   a. Thing
   b. Amount0
   c. Undefined
   d. Undefined

34. In mathematics and the mathematical sciences, a _____ is a fixed, but possibly unspecified, value. This is in contrast to a variable, which is not fixed.
   a. Constant0
   b. Thing
   c. Undefined
   d. Undefined

35. The _____ of measurement are a globally standardized and modernized form of the metric system.
   a. Units0
   b. Thing
   c. Undefined
   d. Undefined

36. In mathematics, an _____, mean, or central tendency of a data set refers to a measure of the "middle" or "expected" value of the data set.
   a. Average0
   b. Concept
   c. Undefined
   d. Undefined

37. In linear algebra, the _____ of an n-by-n square matrix A is defined to be the sum of the elements on the main diagonal of A,

Chapter 3. Further Applications of Derivatives

a. Thing
b. Trace
c. Undefined
d. Undefined

38. A _____ is 360° or 2δ radians.
a. Thing
b. Turn
c. Undefined
d. Undefined

39. _____ is the change in total cost that arises when the quantity produced changes by one unit.
a. Marginal cost
b. Thing
c. Undefined
d. Undefined

40. In mathematics, a _____ is a constant multiplicative factor of a certain object. The object can be such things as a variable, a vector, a function, etc. For example, the _____ of $9x^2$ is 9.
a. Coefficient
b. Thing
c. Undefined
d. Undefined

41. In mathematics, a _____ is a two-dimensional manifold or surface that is perfectly flat.
a. Plane
b. Thing
c. Undefined
d. Undefined

42. In mathematics, a _____ function in the sense of algebraic geometry is an everywhere-defined, polynomial function on an algebraic variety V with values in the field K over which V is defined.
a. Thing
b. Regular
c. Undefined
d. Undefined

43. A _____ is a statement or claimt that a particular event will occur in the future in more certain terms than a forecast.
a. Thing
b. Prediction
c. Undefined
d. Undefined

44. _____ is a a point on a curve at which the tangent crosses the curve itself.
a. Inflection point
b. Thing
c. Undefined
d. Undefined

45. The word _____ means curving in or hollowed inward.
a. Thing
b. Concavity
c. Undefined
d. Undefined

46. In mathematics, the _____ of a coordinate system is the point where the axes of the system intersect.
a. Thing
b. Origin
c. Undefined
d. Undefined

47. _____, from Latin meaning "to make progress", is defined in two different ways. Pure economic _____ is the increase in wealth that an investor has from making an investment, taking into consideration all costs associated with that investment including the opportunity cost of capital.

Chapter 3. Further Applications of Derivatives

a. Profit0
b. Thing
c. Undefined
d. Undefined

48. In business, particularly accounting, a _____ is the time intervals that the accounts, statement, payments, or other calculations cover.
    a. Period0
    b. Thing
    c. Undefined
    d. Undefined

49. A _____ is a special kind of ratio, indicating a relationship between two measurements with different units, such as miles to gallons or cents to pounds.
    a. Thing
    b. Rate0
    c. Undefined
    d. Undefined

50. _____, in economics and political economy, are the distributions or payments awarded to the various suppliers of the factors of production.
    a. Thing
    b. Returns0
    c. Undefined
    d. Undefined

51. A _____ is a function that assigns a number to subsets of a given set.
    a. Thing
    b. Measure0
    c. Undefined
    d. Undefined

52. In combinatorial mathematics, a _____ is an un-ordered collection of unique elements.
    a. Combination0
    b. Concept
    c. Undefined
    d. Undefined

53. A _____ function curves downwards. The graph of a _____ function of one variable remains above its tangents and below its cords.
    a. Convex0
    b. Thing
    c. Undefined
    d. Undefined

54. In Euclidean geometry, a _____ is the set of all points in a plane at a fixed distance, called the radius, from a given point, the center.
    a. Thing
    b. Circle0
    c. Undefined
    d. Undefined

55. In mathematics, _____ growth occurs when the growth rate of a function is always proportional to the function's current size.
    a. Exponential0
    b. Thing
    c. Undefined
    d. Undefined

56. _____ the expected value of a random variable displays the average or central value of the variable. It is a summary value of the distribution of the variable.
    a. Thing
    b. Determining0
    c. Undefined
    d. Undefined

Chapter 3. Further Applications of Derivatives

57. A _____ is a polynomial function of the form f(x) = ax² + bx +c , where a, b, c are real numbers and a , 0.
   a. Event
   b. Quadratic function0
   c. Undefined
   d. Undefined

58. _____ is the process of reducing the number of significant digits in a number.
   a. Rounding0
   b. Concept
   c. Undefined
   d. Undefined

59. _____ is a temperature scale named after the German physicist Daniel Gabriel _____ , who proposed it in 1724.
   a. Fahrenheit0
   b. Thing
   c. Undefined
   d. Undefined

60. In mathematics, there are several meanings of _____ depending on the subject.
   a. Degree0
   b. Thing
   c. Undefined
   d. Undefined

61. _____ is a physical property of a system that underlies the common notions of hot and cold; something that is hotter has the greater _____ .
   a. Thing
   b. Temperature0
   c. Undefined
   d. Undefined

62. _____ is a synonym for information.
   a. Thing
   b. Data0
   c. Undefined
   d. Undefined

63. _____ has many meanings, most of which simply .
   a. Thing
   b. Power0
   c. Undefined
   d. Undefined

64. The term _____ refers to the largest and the smallest element of a set.
   a. Thing
   b. Extreme value0
   c. Undefined
   d. Undefined

65. _____ whose original name was Aristocles, was an ancient Greek philosopher, the second of the great trio of ancient Greeks –succeeding Socrates and preceeding Aristotle– who between them laid the philosophical foundations of Western culture.
   a. Person
   b. Plato0
   c. Undefined
   d. Undefined

66. In geometry, an _____ is a point at which a line segment or ray terminates.
   a. Endpoint0
   b. Thing
   c. Undefined
   d. Undefined

67. A _____ is a function for which, intuitively, small changes in the input result in small changes in the output.

Chapter 3. Further Applications of Derivatives

a. Event
b. Continuous function0
c. Undefined
d. Undefined

68. In mathematics, a _____ is an expression that is constructed from one or more variables and constants, using only the operations of addition, subtraction, multiplication, and constant positive whole number exponents. is a _____. Note in particular that division by an expression containing a variable is not in general allowed in polynomials. [1]
a. Thing
b. Polynomial0
c. Undefined
d. Undefined

69. _____ is the state of being greater than any finite real or natural number, however large.
a. Infinite0
b. Thing
c. Undefined
d. Undefined

70. The _____ are the only integral domain whose positive elements are well-ordered, and in which order is preserved by addition. Like the natural numbers, the _____ form a countably infinite set. The set of all _____ is usually denoted in mathematics by a boldface Z.
a. Thing
b. Integers0
c. Undefined
d. Undefined

71. In mathematics, two quantities are called _____ if they vary in such a way that one of the quantities is a constant multiple of the other, or equivalently if they have a constant ratio.
a. Proportional0
b. Thing
c. Undefined
d. Undefined

72. _____ is a special mathematical relationship between two quantities.Two quantities are called proportional if they vary in such a way that one of the quantities is a constant multiple of the other, or equivalently if they have a constant ratio.
a. Thing
b. Proportionality0
c. Undefined
d. Undefined

73. In plane geometry, a _____ is a polygon with four equal sides, four right angles, and parallel opposite sides. In algebra, the _____ of a number is that number multiplied by itself.
a. Thing
b. Square0
c. Undefined
d. Undefined

74. In mathematics, a _____ of a number x is a number r such that $r^2 = x$, or in words, a number r whose square (the result of multiplying the number by itself) is x.
a. Square root0
b. Thing
c. Undefined
d. Undefined

75. In mathematics, a _____ of a complex-valued function f is a member x of the domain of f such that f(x) vanishes at x, that is, x : f (x) = 0.
a. Thing
b. Root0
c. Undefined
d. Undefined

76. _____ is the symbol used to indicate the nth root of a number

42 Chapter 3. Further Applications of Derivatives

a. Radical0
b. Thing
c. Undefined
d. Undefined

77. In mathematics, a _____ is the result of multiplying, or an expression that identifies factors to be multiplied.
a. Thing
b. Product0
c. Undefined
d. Undefined

78. A _____ is an individual or household that purchases and uses goods and services generated within the economy.
a. Consumer0
b. Thing
c. Undefined
d. Undefined

79. Fixed costs are expenses whose total does not change in proportion to the activity of a business.Unit fixed costs decline with volume following a retangular hyperbola as the volume of production.Variable costs by contrast change in relation to the activity of a business such as sales or production volume.Along with variable costs,fixed costs make up one of the two components of total cost. In the most simple production function total cost is equal to fixed costs plus variable costs.In accounting terminology, fixed costs will broadly include all costs which are not included in cost of goods sold, and variable costs are those captured in costs of goods sold. The implicit assumption required to make the equivalence between the accounting and economics terminology is that the accounting period is equal to the period in which fixed costs do not vary in relation to production. In practice, this equivalence does not always hold and depending on the period under consideration by management, some overhead expenses can be adjusted by management, and the specific allocation of each expense to each category will be decided under cost accounting.In business planning and management accounting, usage of the terms fixed costs, variable costs and others will often differ from usage in economics, and may depend on the intended use. For example, costs may be segregated into per unit costs fixed costs per period, and variable costs as a proportion of revenue. Capital expenditures will usually be allocated separately, and depending on the purpose, a portion may be regularly allocated to expenses as depreciation and amortization and seen as a _____ per period, or the entire amount may be considered upfront fixed costs.
a. Fixed cost0
b. Thing
c. Undefined
d. Undefined

80. _____ are expenses whose total does not change in proportion to the activity of a business, within the relevant time period or scale of production
a. Thing
b. Fixed costs0
c. Undefined
d. Undefined

81. _____ is a business term for the amount of money that a company receives from its activities in a given period, mostly from sales of products and/or services to customers
a. Thing
b. Revenue0
c. Undefined
d. Undefined

82. The plus and _____ signs are mathematical symbols used to represent the notions of positive and negative as well as the operations of addition and subtraction.
a. Minus0
b. Thing
c. Undefined
d. Undefined

83. Equivalence is the condition of being _____ or essentially equal.

Chapter 3. Further Applications of Derivatives

    a. Thing   b. Equivalent0
    c. Undefined   d. Undefined

84. The _____ of a solid object is the three-dimensional concept of how much space it occupies, often quantified numerically.
    a. Thing   b. Volume0
    c. Undefined   d. Undefined

85. In mathematics, the multiplicative inverse of a number x, denoted 1/x or x^{-1}, is the number which, when multiplied by x, yields 1. The multiplicative inverse of x is also called the _____ of x.
    a. Reciprocal0   b. Thing
    c. Undefined   d. Undefined

86. A _____ is the result of the addition of a set of numbers. The numbers may be natural numbers, complex numbers, matrices, or still more complicated objects. An infinite _____ is a subtle procedure known as a series.
    a. Thing   b. Sum0
    c. Undefined   d. Undefined

87. In geometry, a _____ is defined as a quadrilateral where all four of its angles are right angles.
    a. Rectangle0   b. Thing
    c. Undefined   d. Undefined

88. _____ is the distance around a given two-dimensional object. As a general rule, the _____ of a polygon can always be calculated by adding all the length of the sides together. So, the formula for triangles is P = a + b + c, where a, b and c stand for each side of it. For quadrilaterals the equation is P = a + b + c + d. For equilateral polygons, P = na, where n is the number of sides and a is the side length.
    a. Thing   b. Perimeter0
    c. Undefined   d. Undefined

89. _____ is the force that opposes the relative motion or tendency toward such motion of two surfaces in contact.
    a. Thing   b. Friction0
    c. Undefined   d. Undefined

90. _____ of an object is its speed in a particular direction.
    a. Velocity0   b. Thing
    c. Undefined   d. Undefined

91. In classical geometry, a _____ of a circle or sphere is any line segment from its center to its boundary. By extension, the _____ of a circle or sphere is the length of any such segment. The _____ is half the diameter. In science and engineering the term _____ of curvature is commonly used as a synonym for _____.
    a. Radius0   b. Thing
    c. Undefined   d. Undefined

92. _____ is the ability to hold, receive or absorb, or a measure thereof, similar to the concept of volume.

Chapter 3. Further Applications of Derivatives

    a. Capacity0   b. Concept
    c. Undefined   d. Undefined

93. _____ is process in which two clone daughter cells are produced by the cell division of one bacterium.
    a. Thing   b. Bacterial growth0
    c. Undefined   d. Undefined

94. The word _____ comes from the Latin word linearis, which means created by lines.
    a. Linear0   b. Thing
    c. Undefined   d. Undefined

95. _____ is a regression method that models the relationship between a dependent variable Y, independent variables Xp, and a random term å.
    a. Thing   b. Linear regression0
    c. Undefined   d. Undefined

96. In mathematics, _____ refers to the rewriting of an expression into a simpler form.
    a. Thing   b. Reduction0
    c. Undefined   d. Undefined

97. In mathematics, _____ expressions is used to reduce the expression into the lowest possible term.
    a. Simplifying0   b. Thing
    c. Undefined   d. Undefined

98. A _____ is a symbolic representation denoting a quantity or expression. It often represents an "unknown" quantity that has the potential to change.
    a. Variable0   b. Thing
    c. Undefined   d. Undefined

99. A _____ is a three-dimensional solid object bounded by six square faces, facets, or sides, with three meeting at each vertex.
    a. Thing   b. Cube0
    c. Undefined   d. Undefined

100. A _____ of a number is a number a such that $a^3 = x$.
    a. Cube root0   b. Thing
    c. Undefined   d. Undefined

101. A _____ is a consumption tax charged at the point of purchase for certain goods and services.
    a. Sales tax0   b. Thing
    c. Undefined   d. Undefined

102. In epidemiology, an _____ is a disease that appears as new cases in a given human population, during a given period, at a rate that substantially exceeds with is "expected," based on recent experience.

Chapter 3. Further Applications of Derivatives

a. Epidemic0   b. Thing
c. Undefined   d. Undefined

103. _____ is an economics theory, that refers to individuals or societies gaining the maximum amount out of the resources they have available to them.
    a. Thing   b. Maximization0
    c. Undefined   d. Undefined

104. _____ is a list of goods and materials, or those goods and materials themselves, held available in stock by a business
    a. Inventory0   b. Thing
    c. Undefined   d. Undefined

105. In mathematics, a _____ can mean either an element of the set {1, 2, 3, ...} (i.e the positive integers) or an element of the set {0, 1, 2, 3, ...} (i.e. the non-negative integers).
    a. Concept   b. Whole number0
    c. Undefined   d. Undefined

106. _____ is the application of tools and a processing medium to the transformation of raw materials into finished goods for sale.
    a. Thing   b. Manufacturing0
    c. Undefined   d. Undefined

107. In economics, supply and _____ describe market relations between prospective sellers and buyers of a good.
    a. Demand0   b. Thing
    c. Undefined   d. Undefined

108. In mathematics, a subset of Euclidean space R^n is called _____ if it is closed and bounded.
    a. Compact0   b. Thing
    c. Undefined   d. Undefined

109. _____ is to give an equation $R(x,y) = S(x,y)$ that at least in part has the same graph as $y = f(x)$.
    a. Thing   b. Implicit differentiation0
    c. Undefined   d. Undefined

110. _____, a field in mathematics, is the study of how functions change when their inputs change. The primary object of study in _____ is the derivative.
    a. Thing   b. Differential calculus0
    c. Undefined   d. Undefined

111. In differential calculus, _____ problems involve finding the rate at which a quantity is changing by relating that quantity to other quantities whose rates of change are known.
    a. Related rates0   b. Thing
    c. Undefined   d. Undefined

112. The _____ governs the differentiation of products of differentiable functions.

a. Product rule0
b. Thing
c. Undefined
d. Undefined

113. _____ is a method for differentiating expressions involving exponentiation the power operation.
a. Power rule0
b. Thing
c. Undefined
d. Undefined

114. In physics, _____ are surface waves on a liquid with wavelengths so short that the liquid's motion is governed almost entirely by surface tension forces.
a. Ripples0
b. Thing
c. Undefined
d. Undefined

115. In mathematics, a _____ is a number which can be expressed as a ratio of two integers. Non-integer rational numbers (commonly called fractions) are usually written as the vulgar fraction a / b, where b is not zero.
a. Rational Number0
b. Concept
c. Undefined
d. Undefined

116. In mathematics, a _____ is the set of all points in three-dimensional space (R^3) which are at distance r from a fixed point of that space, where r is a positive real number called the radius of the _____. The fixed point is called the center or centre, and is not part of the _____ itself.
a. Thing
b. Sphere0
c. Undefined
d. Undefined

117. _____ is the flow of blood in the cardiovascular system.
a. Blood flow0
b. Thing
c. Undefined
d. Undefined

118. In mathematics, an _____ .
a. Thing
b. Ellipse0
c. Undefined
d. Undefined

119. A _____ is a unit of length, usually used to measure distance, in a number of different systems, including Imperial units, United States customary units and Norwegian/Swedish mil. Its size can vary from system to system, but in each is between 1 and 10 kilometers. In contemporary English contexts _____ refers to either:
a. Thing
b. Mile0
c. Undefined
d. Undefined

120. In computer science, an _____ is the problem of finding the best solution from all feasible solutions.
a. Optimization problem0
b. Thing
c. Undefined
d. Undefined

121. In mathematics, an _____ is any of the arguments, i.e. "inputs", to a function. Thus if we have a function f(x), then x is a _____.
a. Thing
b. Independent variable0
c. Undefined
d. Undefined

Chapter 3. Further Applications of Derivatives

122. A _____ is the sum of the elements of a sequence.
   a. Series0
   b. Thing
   c. Undefined
   d. Undefined

123. Two mathematical objects are equal if and only if they are precisely the same in every way. This defines a binary relation, _____, denoted by the sign of _____ "=" in such a way that the statement "x = y" means that x and y are equal.
   a. Equality0
   b. Thing
   c. Undefined
   d. Undefined

124. An _____ is a combination of numbers, operators, grouping symbols and/or free variables and bound variables arranged in a meaningful way which can be evaluated..
   a. Thing
   b. Expression0
   c. Undefined
   d. Undefined

125. _____ is the name for any one of many units of measure used by various ancient peoples and is among the first recorded units of length.
   a. Cubit0
   b. Thing
   c. Undefined
   d. Undefined

126. _____ is mass m per unit volume V.
   a. Density0
   b. Thing
   c. Undefined
   d. Undefined

127. Regrouping is the act of putting ones into groups of 10. For example, the 1 on the far right of 131 would be denoted _____ if the digit of the number being subtracted is larger than 1, such as 131-99.
   a. By 100
   b. Thing
   c. Undefined
   d. Undefined

128. _____ asserts that the maximum output of a technologically-determined production process is a mathematical function of input factors of production.
   a. Thing
   b. Production function0
   c. Undefined
   d. Undefined

129. _____ is one of the most important functions in mathematics. A function commonly used to study growth and decay
   a. Thing
   b. Exponential function0
   c. Undefined
   d. Undefined

130. In economics and business studies, the _____ is an elasticity that measures the nature and degree of the relationship between changes in quantity demanded of a good and changes in its price.
   a. Elasticity of demand0
   b. Thing
   c. Undefined
   d. Undefined

131. The act of _____ is the calculated approximation of a result which is usable even if input data may be incomplete, uncertain, or noisy.

Chapter 3. Further Applications of Derivatives

a. Thing
b. Estimating0
c. Undefined
d. Undefined

132. In geometry and physics, _____ are half-lines that continue forever in one direction.
a. Rays0
b. Thing
c. Undefined
d. Undefined

133. _____ numerals are a numeral system originating in ancient Rome, adapted from Etruscan numerals.
a. Thing
b. Roman0
c. Undefined
d. Undefined

134. _____ is a subset of a population.
a. Sample0
b. Thing
c. Undefined
d. Undefined

135. A _____ is a type of particle detector that measures ionizing radiation.
a. Geiger counter0
b. Thing
c. Undefined
d. Undefined

136. A _____ is a quantity that denotes the proportional amount or magnitude of one quantity relative to another.
a. Ratio0
b. Thing
c. Undefined
d. Undefined

Chapter 4. Exponential and Logarithmic Functions

1. A _____ is a symbolic representation denoting a quantity or expression. It often represents an "unknown" quantity that has the potential to change.
   a. Variable0
   b. Thing
   c. Undefined
   d. Undefined

2. In mathematics, _____ growth occurs when the growth rate of a function is always proportional to the function's current size.
   a. Exponential0
   b. Thing
   c. Undefined
   d. Undefined

3. _____ is one of the most important functions in mathematics. A function commonly used to study growth and decay
   a. Thing
   b. Exponential function0
   c. Undefined
   d. Undefined

4. A _____ is a three-dimensional geometric shape formed by straight lines through a fixed point (vertex) to the points of a fixed curve (directrix)
   a. Cone0
   b. Concept
   c. Undefined
   d. Undefined

5. _____ is a term used in accounting, economics and finance with reference to the fact that assets with finite lives lose value over time.
   a. Depreciation0
   b. Thing
   c. Undefined
   d. Undefined

6. The mathematical concept of a _____ expresses the intuitive idea of deterministic dependence between two quantities, one of which is viewed as primary and the other as secondary. A _____ then is a way to associate a unique output for each input of a specified type, for example, a real number or an element of a given set.
   a. Function0
   b. Thing
   c. Undefined
   d. Undefined

7. In mathematics, the concept of a _____ tries to capture the intuitive idea of a geometrical one-dimensional and continuous object. A simple example is the circle.
   a. Thing
   b. Curve0
   c. Undefined
   d. Undefined

8. In mathematics, _____ is a part of the set theoretic notion of function.
   a. Image0
   b. Thing
   c. Undefined
   d. Undefined

9. A _____ are accounts maintained by commercial banks, savings and loan associations, credit unions, and mutual savings banks that pay interest but can not be used directly as money by, for example, writing a cheque.
   a. Savings account0
   b. Thing
   c. Undefined
   d. Undefined

10. In sociology and biology a _____ is the collection of people or organisms of a particular species living in a given geographic area or space, usually measured by a census.

Chapter 4. Exponential and Logarithmic Functions

    a. Population0   b. Thing
    c. Undefined   d. Undefined

11. _____ is often used to describe the measurement of the steepness, incline, gradient, or grade of a straight line. The _____ is defined as the ratio of the "rise" divided by the "run" between two points on a line, or in other words, the ratio of the altitude change to the horizontal distance between any two points on the line.
    a. Thing   b. Slope0
    c. Undefined   d. Undefined

12. _____ is the fee paid on borrowed money.
    a. Thing   b. Interest0
    c. Undefined   d. Undefined

13. _____ interest refers to the fact that whenever interest is calculated, it is based not only on the original principal, but also on any unpaid interest that has been added to the principal.
    a. Compound0   b. Thing
    c. Undefined   d. Undefined

14. _____ refers to the fact that whenever interest is calculated, it is based not only on the original principal, but also on any unpaid interest that has been added to the principal. The more frequently interest is compounded, the faster the balance grows.
    a. Compound interest0   b. Concept
    c. Undefined   d. Undefined

15. A _____ is a special kind of ratio, indicating a relationship between two measurements with different units, such as miles to gallons or cents to pounds.
    a. Rate0   b. Thing
    c. Undefined   d. Undefined

16. In business, particularly accounting, a _____ is the time intervals that the accounts, statement, payments, or other calculations cover.
    a. Thing   b. Period0
    c. Undefined   d. Undefined

17. An _____ is the fee paid on borrow money.
    a. Concept   b. Interest rate0
    c. Undefined   d. Undefined

18. The _____, the average in everyday English, which is also called the arithmetic _____ (and is distinguished from the geometric _____ or harmonic _____). The average is also called the sample _____. The expected value of a random variable, which is also called the population _____.
    a. Thing   b. Mean0
    c. Undefined   d. Undefined

19. _____ is a kind of property which exists as magnitude or multitude. It is among the basic classes of things along with quality, substance, change, and relation.

Chapter 4. Exponential and Logarithmic Functions

a. Amount0
b. Thing
c. Undefined
d. Undefined

20. A _____ is the result of the addition of a set of numbers. The numbers may be natural numbers, complex numbers, matrices, or still more complicated objects. An infinite _____ is a subtle procedure known as a series.
   a. Sum0
   b. Thing
   c. Undefined
   d. Undefined

21. _____ of a single or multiple future payments is the nominal amounts of money to change hands at some future date, discounted to account for the time value of money, and other factors such as investment risk.
   a. Present value0
   b. Thing
   c. Undefined
   d. Undefined

22. _____ measures the nominal future sum of money that a given sum of money is "worth" at a specified time in the future assuming a certain interest rate; this value does not include corrections for inflation or other factors that affect the true value of money in the future.
   a. Future value0
   b. Thing
   c. Undefined
   d. Undefined

23. _____ are economic entities that give rise to future economic benefit and is controlled by the entity as a result of past transaction or other events
   a. Thing
   b. Asset0
   c. Undefined
   d. Undefined

24. Equivalence is the condition of being _____ or essentially equal.
   a. Thing
   b. Equivalent0
   c. Undefined
   d. Undefined

25. In banking and accountancy, the outstanding _____ is the amount of money owned, or due, that remains in a deposit account or a loan account at a given date, after all past remittances, payments and withdrawal have been accounted for.
   a. Thing
   b. Balance0
   c. Undefined
   d. Undefined

26. A _____ function is a function for which, intuitively, small changes in the input result in small changes in the output.
   a. Event
   b. Continuous0
   c. Undefined
   d. Undefined

27. _____ is the state of being greater than any finite number, however large.
   a. Infinity0
   b. Thing
   c. Undefined
   d. Undefined

28. In statistics the _____ of an event i is the number n_i of times the event occurred in the experiment or the study. These frequencies are often graphically represented in histograms.

Chapter 4. Exponential and Logarithmic Functions

a. Frequency0
c. Undefined
b. Concept
d. Undefined

29. _____ generally derives from name. A _____ quantity e.g., length, diameter, volume, voltage, value is generally the quantity according to which some item has been named or is generally referred to.
   a. Nominal0
   b. Thing
   c. Undefined
   d. Undefined

30. In botany, _____ are above-ground plant organs specialized for photosynthesis. Their characteristics are typically analyzed by using Fiobonacci's sequences.
   a. Thing
   b. Leaves0
   c. Undefined
   d. Undefined

31. _____ is an expression of the effective interest rate that will be paid on a loan, taking into account one-time fees and standardizing the way the rate is expressed.
   a. Annual percentage rate0
   b. Thing
   c. Undefined
   d. Undefined

32. _____ has many meanings, most of which simply .
   a. Power0
   b. Thing
   c. Undefined
   d. Undefined

33. In mathematics, _____ are the intuitive idea of a geometrical one-dimensional and continuous object.
   a. Curves0
   b. Thing
   c. Undefined
   d. Undefined

34. In mathematics and the mathematical sciences, a _____ is a fixed, but possibly unspecified, value. This is in contrast to a variable, which is not fixed.
   a. Thing
   b. Constant0
   c. Undefined
   d. Undefined

35. _____ is the process of reducing the number of significant digits in a number.
   a. Concept
   b. Rounding0
   c. Undefined
   d. Undefined

36. A _____ is a type of debt. All material things can be lent but this article focuses exclusively on monetary loans. Like all debt instruments, a _____ entails the redistribution of financial assets over time, between the lender and the borrower.
   a. Thing
   b. Loan0
   c. Undefined
   d. Undefined

37. A _____ is a negotiable instrument instructing a financial institution to pay a specific amount of a specific currency from a specific demand account held in the maker/depositor's name with that institution. Both the maker and payee may be natural persons or legal entities.

Chapter 4. Exponential and Logarithmic Functions

a. Check0
b. Thing
c. Undefined
d. Undefined

38. In mathematics, a _____ function in the sense of algebraic geometry is an everywhere-defined, polynomial function on an algebraic variety V with values in the field K over which V is defined.
a. Thing
b. Regular0
c. Undefined
d. Undefined

39. A _____ is an individual or household that purchases and uses goods and services generated within the economy.
a. Consumer0
b. Thing
c. Undefined
d. Undefined

40. _____ finance, in finance, a debt security, issued by Issuer
a. Bond0
b. Thing
c. Undefined
d. Undefined

41. The _____ is the total number of human beings alive on the planet Earth at a given time.
a. World population0
b. Thing
c. Undefined
d. Undefined

42. The population _____ is the total number of human beings alive on the planet Earth at a given time.
a. Of the world0
b. Thing
c. Undefined
d. Undefined

43. _____ is a special mathematical relationship between two quantities. Two quantities are called proportional if they vary in such a way that one of the quantities is a constant multiple of the other, or equivalently if they have a constant ratio.
a. Proportionality0
b. Thing
c. Undefined
d. Undefined

44. _____ is electromagnetic radiation with a wavelength that is visible to the eye (visible _____) or, in a technical or scientific context, electromagnetic radiation of any wavelength.
a. Thing
b. Light0
c. Undefined
d. Undefined

45. _____ is process in which two clone daughter cells are produced by the cell division of one bacterium.
a. Bacterial growth0
b. Thing
c. Undefined
d. Undefined

46. In mathematics, a _____ is the result of multiplying, or an expression that identifies factors to be multiplied.
a. Thing
b. Product0
c. Undefined
d. Undefined

47. In a mathematical proof or a syllogism, a _____ is a statement that is the logical consequence of preceding statements.

Chapter 4. Exponential and Logarithmic Functions

a. Conclusion0
b. Concept
c. Undefined
d. Undefined

48. _____ is a way of expressing a number as a fraction of 100 per cent meaning "per hundred".
   a. Percent0
   b. Thing
   c. Undefined
   d. Undefined

49. _____ is a state located in the southern and southwestern regions of the United States of America.
   a. Thing
   b. Texas0
   c. Undefined
   d. Undefined

50. _____ is the shape of a hanging flexible chain or cable when supported at its ends and acted upon by a uniform gravitational force. The chain is steepest near the points of suspension because this part of the chain has the most weight pulling down on it. Toward the bottom, the slope of the chain decreases because the chain is supporting less weight.
   a. Thing
   b. Catenary0
   c. Undefined
   d. Undefined

51. The Jefferson National Expansion Memorial or _____ is located in St. Louis, Missouri near the start of the Lewis and Clark Expedition. It was designated as a National Memorial by Executive Order 7523, on December 21, 1935, and is maintained by the National Park Service ..
   a. Gateway Arch0
   b. Place
   c. Undefined
   d. Undefined

52. In geometry, the _____ of an object is a point in some sense in the middle of the object.
   a. Thing
   b. Center0
   c. Undefined
   d. Undefined

53. _____ is a temperature scale named after the German physicist Daniel Gabriel _____ , who proposed it in 1724.
   a. Thing
   b. Fahrenheit0
   c. Undefined
   d. Undefined

54. In mathematics, there are several meanings of _____ depending on the subject.
   a. Thing
   b. Degree0
   c. Undefined
   d. Undefined

55. _____ is a physical property of a system that underlies the common notions of hot and cold; something that is hotter has the greater _____ .
   a. Temperature0
   b. Thing
   c. Undefined
   d. Undefined

56. The _____ of measurement are a globally standardized and modernized form of the metric system.
   a. Units0
   b. Thing
   c. Undefined
   d. Undefined

Chapter 4. Exponential and Logarithmic Functions

57. In the scientific method, an _____ (Latin: ex-+-periri, "of (or from) trying"), is a set of actions and observations, performed in the context of solving a particular problem or question, in order to support or falsify a hypothesis or research concerning phenomena.
   a. Experiment0
   b. Thing
   c. Undefined
   d. Undefined

58. In epidemiology, an _____ is a disease that appears as new cases in a given human population, during a given period, at a rate that substantially exceeds with is "expected," based on recent experience.
   a. Thing
   b. Epidemic0
   c. Undefined
   d. Undefined

59. _____ or investing is a term with several closely-related meanings in business management, finance and economics, related to saving or deferring consumption.
   a. Thing
   b. Investment0
   c. Undefined
   d. Undefined

60. In mathematics, a _____ of a number x is the exponent y of the power by such that $x = b^y$. The value used for the base b must be neither 0 nor 1, nor a root of 1 in the case of the extension to complex numbers, and is typically 10, e, or 2.
   a. Thing
   b. Logarithm0
   c. Undefined
   d. Undefined

61. A _____ is a number, figure, or indicator that appears below the normal line of type, typically used in a formula, mathematical expression, or description of a chemical compound.
   a. Thing
   b. Subscript0
   c. Undefined
   d. Undefined

62. _____ is the logarithm to the base e, where e is an irrational constant approximately equal to 2.718281828459.
   a. Natural logarithm0
   b. Thing
   c. Undefined
   d. Undefined

63. John _____ of Merchistoun , nicknamed Marvellous Merchistoun, was a Scottish mathematician, physicist, astronomer/astrologer and 8th Laird of Merchistoun. He is most remembered as the inventor of logarithms and _____'s bones, and for popularizing the use of the decimal point.
   a. Person
   b. Napier0
   c. Undefined
   d. Undefined

64. _____ of Nerchistoun, nicknamed Marvellous Merchistoun, was a Scottish mathematician, physicist, astronomer/astrologer and 8th Laird of Merchistoun.
   a. John Napier0
   b. Person
   c. Undefined
   d. Undefined

65. The decimal separator is a symbol used to mark the boundary between the integral and the fractional parts of a decimal numeral. Terms implying the symbol used are _____ and decimal comma.
   a. Concept
   b. Decimal point0
   c. Undefined
   d. Undefined

Chapter 4. Exponential and Logarithmic Functions

66. _____ is a mathematical operation, written a^n, involving two numbers, the base a and the exponent n.
    a. Exponentiating0   b. Thing
    c. Undefined   d. Undefined

67. _____ is a mathematical operation, written a^n, involving two numbers, the base a and the exponent n.
    a. Exponentiation0   b. Thing
    c. Undefined   d. Undefined

68. In mathematics, a _____ is the end result of a division problem. It can also be expressed as the number of times the divisor divides into the dividend.
    a. Thing   b. Quotient0
    c. Undefined   d. Undefined

69. In mathematics, _____ expressions is used to reduce the expression into the lowest possible term.
    a. Thing   b. Simplifying0
    c. Undefined   d. Undefined

70. _____ are the basic objects of study in graph theory. Informally speaking, a graph is a set of objects called points, nodes, or vertices connected by links called lines or edges.
    a. Graphs0   b. Thing
    c. Undefined   d. Undefined

71. _____ element of an element x with respect to a binary operation * with identity element e is an element y such that x * y = y * x = e. In particular,
    a. Inverse0   b. Thing
    c. Undefined   d. Undefined

72. An _____ is a function which does the reverse of a given function.
    a. Thing   b. Inverse function0
    c. Undefined   d. Undefined

73. In mathematics, a _____ is an n-tuple with n being 3.
    a. Thing   b. Triple0
    c. Undefined   d. Undefined

74. A _____ of a number is the product of that number with any integer.
    a. Thing   b. Multiple0
    c. Undefined   d. Undefined

75. Initial objects are also called _____, and terminal objects are also called final.
    a. Thing   b. Coterminal0
    c. Undefined   d. Undefined

76. A _____ is a function that assigns a number to subsets of a given set.

Chapter 4. Exponential and Logarithmic Functions

a. Measure0
b. Thing
c. Undefined
d. Undefined

77. _____ (or proportionality) are two quantities that vary in such a way that one of the quatities is a constant multiple of the other, or equivalently if they have a constant ratio.
   a. Proportions0
   b. Thing
   c. Undefined
   d. Undefined

78. _____ is the property of a physical object that quantifies the amount of matter and energy it is equivalent to.
   a. Thing
   b. Mass0
   c. Undefined
   d. Undefined

79. _____ is the net action of matter particles or molecules, heat, momentum, or light whose end is to minimize a concentration gradient
   a. Diffusion0
   b. Thing
   c. Undefined
   d. Undefined

80. In mathematics, the _____ of a function is the set of all "output" values produced by that function. Given a function $f : A \to B$, the _____ of f, is defined to be the set $\{x \in B : x = f(a)$ for some $a \in A\}$.
   a. Range0
   b. Thing
   c. Undefined
   d. Undefined

81. In mathematics, a _____ of a k-place relation $L \subseteq X_1 \times \ldots \times X_k$ is one of the sets X_j, $1 \leq j \leq k$. In the special case where k = 2 and $L \subseteq X_1 \times X_2$ is a function $L : X_1 \to X_2$, it is conventional to refer to X_1 as the _____ of the function and to refer to X_2 as the codomain of the function.
   a. Domain0
   b. Thing
   c. Undefined
   d. Undefined

82. _____ is a state in the southern region of the United States of America and was one of the original Thirteen Colonies that revolted against British rule in the American Revolution.
   a. Thing
   b. Georgia0
   c. Undefined
   d. Undefined

83. _____ is change in population over time, and can be quantified as the change in the number of individuals in a population per unit time.
   a. Thing
   b. Population growth0
   c. Undefined
   d. Undefined

84. _____ are a measure of time.
   a. Minutes0
   b. Thing
   c. Undefined
   d. Undefined

85. _____ is a subset of a population.
   a. Thing
   b. Sample0
   c. Undefined
   d. Undefined

Chapter 4. Exponential and Logarithmic Functions

86. _____ are waste types containing radioactive chemical elements that do not have a practical purpose.
   a. Radioactive waste0
   b. Thing
   c. Undefined
   d. Undefined

87. Acid _____ ratio measures the ability of a company to use its near cash or quick assets to immediately extinguish its current liabilities.
   a. Thing
   b. Test0
   c. Undefined
   d. Undefined

88. In mainstream economics, the word _____ refers to a general rise in prices measured against a standard level of purchasing power.
   a. Thing
   b. Inflation0
   c. Undefined
   d. Undefined

89. The _____ is a measurement of how a function changes when the values of its inputs change.
   a. Thing
   b. Derivative0
   c. Undefined
   d. Undefined

90. The _____ governs the differentiation of products of differentiable functions.
   a. Thing
   b. Product rule0
   c. Undefined
   d. Undefined

91. _____, a field in mathematics, is the study of how functions change when their inputs change. The primary object of study in _____ is the derivative.
   a. Differential calculus0
   b. Thing
   c. Undefined
   d. Undefined

92. The _____ is a method of finding the derivative of a function that is the quotient of two other functions for which derivatives exist.
   a. Quotient rule0
   b. Thing
   c. Undefined
   d. Undefined

93. _____ is a method for differentiating expressions involving exponentiation the power operation.
   a. Power rule0
   b. Thing
   c. Undefined
   d. Undefined

94. In mathematics, two quantities are called _____ if they vary in such a way that one of the quantities is a constant multiple of the other, or equivalently if they have a constant ratio.
   a. Proportional0
   b. Thing
   c. Undefined
   d. Undefined

95. In economics, supply and _____ describe market relations between prospective sellers and buyers of a good.
   a. Demand0
   b. Thing
   c. Undefined
   d. Undefined

Chapter 4. Exponential and Logarithmic Functions

96. _____ is a mathematical subject that includes the study of limits, derivatives, integrals, and power series and constitutes a major part of modern university curriculum.
   a. Calculus0
   b. Thing
   c. Undefined
   d. Undefined

97. _____ is a point on the domain of a function
   a. Critical point0
   b. Thing
   c. Undefined
   d. Undefined

98. _____ is a a point on a curve at which the tangent crosses the curve itself.
   a. Thing
   b. Inflection point0
   c. Undefined
   d. Undefined

99. A _____ is a simplified and structured visual representation of concepts, ideas, constructions, relations, statistical data, anatomy etc used in all aspects of human activities to visualize and clarify the topic.
   a. Diagram0
   b. Thing
   c. Undefined
   d. Undefined

100. _____ is a mathematical science pertaining to the collection, analysis, interpretation or explanation, and presentation of data. It is applicable to a wide variety of academic disciplines, from the physical and social sciences to the humanities.
   a. Thing
   b. Statistics0
   c. Undefined
   d. Undefined

101. A _____ is a statement or claimt that a particular event will occur in the future in more certain terms than a forecast.
   a. Prediction0
   b. Thing
   c. Undefined
   d. Undefined

102. In mathematics, a _____ number is a number which can be expressed as a ratio of two integers. Non-integer _____ numbers (commonly called fractions) are usually written as the vulgar fraction a / b, where b is not zero.
   a. Rational0
   b. Thing
   c. Undefined
   d. Undefined

103. An _____ is a combination of numbers, operators, grouping symbols and/or free variables and bound variables arranged in a meaningful way which can be evaluated..
   a. Thing
   b. Expression0
   c. Undefined
   d. Undefined

104. _____ is to give an equation R(x,y) = S(x,y) that at least in part has the same graph as y = f(x).
   a. Thing
   b. Implicit differentiation0
   c. Undefined
   d. Undefined

105. _____ is a business term for the amount of money that a company receives from its activities in a given period, mostly from sales of products and/or services to customers

Chapter 4. Exponential and Logarithmic Functions

a. Revenue0
c. Undefined
b. Thing
d. Undefined

106. The _____ of a ring R is defined to be the smallest positive integer n such that $n\,a = 0$, for all a in R.
    a. Characteristic0
    b. Thing
    c. Undefined
    d. Undefined

107. _____ is the flow of blood in the cardiovascular system.
    a. Thing
    b. Blood flow0
    c. Undefined
    d. Undefined

108. _____ is defined as the rate of change or derivative with respect to time of velocity.
    a. Thing
    b. Acceleration0
    c. Undefined
    d. Undefined

109. _____ of an object is its speed in a particular direction.
    a. Velocity0
    b. Thing
    c. Undefined
    d. Undefined

110. The metre (or _____, see spelling differences) is a measure of length. It is the basic unit of length in the metric system and in the International System of Units (SI), used around the world for general and scientific purposes.
    a. Meter0
    b. Concept
    c. Undefined
    d. Undefined

111. A _____ is a unit of length, usually used to measure distance, in a number of different systems, including Imperial units, United States customary units and Norwegian/Swedish mil. Its size can vary from system to system, but in each is between 1 and 10 kilometers. In contemporary English contexts _____ refers to either:
    a. Mile0
    b. Thing
    c. Undefined
    d. Undefined

112. In economics and business studies, the _____ is an elasticity that measures the nature and degree of the relationship between changes in quantity demanded of a good and changes in its price.
    a. Elasticity of demand0
    b. Thing
    c. Undefined
    d. Undefined

113. A _____ is a quantity that denotes the proportional amount or magnitude of one quantity relative to another.
    a. Thing
    b. Ratio0
    c. Undefined
    d. Undefined

114. In economics _____ means before deductions brutto, e.g. _____ domestic or national product, or _____ profit or income
    a. Thing
    b. Gross0
    c. Undefined
    d. Undefined

115. A _____ is 360° or 2δ radians.

Chapter 4. Exponential and Logarithmic Functions

a. Thing
c. Undefined
b. Turn0
d. Undefined

116. In mathematics, the additive inverse, or _____ of a number n is the number that, when added to n, yields zero. The additive inverse of n is denoted −n. For example, 7 is −7, because 7 + (−7) = 0, and the additive inverse of −0.3 is 0.3, because −0.3 + 0.3 = 0.
a. Thing
c. Undefined
b. Opposite0
d. Undefined

117. In mathematics, the _____ of a number n is the number that, when added to n, yields zero. The _____ of n is denoted −n. For example, 7 is −7, because 7 + (−7) = 0, and the _____ of −0.3 is 0.3, because −0.3 + 0.3 = 0.
a. Additive inverse0
c. Undefined
b. Thing
d. Undefined

118. In common philosophical language, a proposition or _____, is the content of an assertion, that is, it is true-or-false and defined by the meaning of a particular piece of language.
a. Concept
c. Undefined
b. Statement0
d. Undefined

119. _____ can be defined as the graph depicting the relationship between the price of a certain commodity, and the amount of it that consumers are willing and able to purchase at that given price demand.
a. Demand curve0
c. Undefined
b. Thing
d. Undefined

120. The payment of _____ as remuneration for services rendered or products sold is a common way to reward sales people.
a. Commission0
c. Undefined
b. Thing
d. Undefined

121. U.S. liquid _____ is legally defined as 231 cubic inches, and is equal to 3.785411784 litres or abotu 0.13368 cubic feet. This is the most common definition of a _____. The U.S. fluid ounce is defined as 1/128 of a U.S. _____.
a. Thing
c. Undefined
b. Gallon0
d. Undefined

122. The word _____ comes from the Latin word linearis, which means created by lines.
a. Thing
c. Undefined
b. Linear0
d. Undefined

123. In finance, the _____, the rule of 71, the rule of 70 and the rule of 69.3 all refer to a method for estimating an investment's doubling time, or halving time. These rules apply to exponential growth and decay respectively, and are therefore used for compound interest as opposed to simple interest calculations.
a. Rule of 720
c. Undefined
b. Thing
d. Undefined

Chapter 4. Exponential and Logarithmic Functions

124. An _____ in policy debate is part of a speech which is flagged as not responding to the line-by-line arguments on the flow.
   a. Thing
   b. Overview0
   c. Undefined
   d. Undefined

125. In mathematics, a _____ is an expression that is constructed from one or more variables and constants, using only the operations of addition, subtraction, multiplication, and constant positive whole number exponents. is a _____. Note in particular that division by an expression containing a variable is not in general allowed in polynomials. [1]
   a. Polynomial0
   b. Thing
   c. Undefined
   d. Undefined

126. The _____ is the period of time required for a quantity to double in size or value.
   a. Thing
   b. Doubling time0
   c. Undefined
   d. Undefined

127. _____ is an extension of the concept of a sum.
   a. Definite integral0
   b. Thing
   c. Undefined
   d. Undefined

128. In mathematics, an _____, mean, or central tendency of a data set refers to a measure of the "middle" or "expected" value of the data set.
   a. Concept
   b. Average0
   c. Undefined
   d. Undefined

129. The _____ of a function is an extension of the concept of a sum, and are identified or found through the use of integration.
   a. Thing
   b. Integral0
   c. Undefined
   d. Undefined

130. _____ is a process of combining or accumulating. It may also refer to:
   a. Thing
   b. Integration0
   c. Undefined
   d. Undefined

131. In mathematical analysis, _____ are objects which generalize functions and probability distributions.
   a. Thing
   b. Distribution0
   c. Undefined
   d. Undefined

132. _____ is the level of functional and/or metabolic efficiency of an organism at both the micro level.
   a. Health0
   b. Thing
   c. Undefined
   d. Undefined

Chapter 5. Integration and Its Applications

1. _____ in calculus is primitive or indefinite integral of a function f is a function F whose derivative is equal to f, i.e., F Œ = f. The process of solving for antiderivatives is _____
   a. Thing
   b. Antidifferentiation0
   c. Undefined
   d. Undefined

2. The _____ of a function is an extension of the concept of a sum, and are identified or found through the use of integration.
   a. Integral0
   b. Thing
   c. Undefined
   d. Undefined

3. An _____ of a function f is a function F whose derivative is equal to f, i.e., F' = f.
   a. Antiderivative0
   b. Thing
   c. Undefined
   d. Undefined

4. The _____ is a measurement of how a function changes when the values of its inputs change.
   a. Thing
   b. Derivative0
   c. Undefined
   d. Undefined

5. A _____ is a symbolic representation denoting a quantity or expression. It often represents an "unknown" quantity that has the potential to change.
   a. Thing
   b. Variable0
   c. Undefined
   d. Undefined

6. _____ is a process of combining or accumulating. It may also refer to:
   a. Integration0
   b. Thing
   c. Undefined
   d. Undefined

7. In mathematics and the mathematical sciences, a _____ is a fixed, but possibly unspecified, value. This is in contrast to a variable, which is not fixed.
   a. Thing
   b. Constant0
   c. Undefined
   d. Undefined

8. _____ is a function that extends the concept of an ordinary sum
   a. Thing
   b. Integrand0
   c. Undefined
   d. Undefined

9. _____, a field in mathematics, is the study of how functions change when their inputs change. The primary object of study in _____ is the derivative.
   a. Differential calculus0
   b. Thing
   c. Undefined
   d. Undefined

10. A _____ is a negotiable instrument instructing a financial institution to pay a specific amount of a specific currency from a specific demand account held in the maker/depositor's name with that institution. Both the maker and payee may be natural persons or legal entities.
    a. Thing
    b. Check0
    c. Undefined
    d. Undefined

Chapter 5. Integration and Its Applications

11. _____ has many meanings, most of which simply .
    a. Power0
    b. Thing
    c. Undefined
    d. Undefined

12. _____ is a method for differentiating expressions involving exponentiation the power operation.
    a. Power rule0
    b. Thing
    c. Undefined
    d. Undefined

13. The mathematical concept of a _____ expresses the intuitive idea of deterministic dependence between two quantities, one of which is viewed as primary and the other as secondary. A _____ then is a way to associate a unique output for each input of a specified type, for example, a real number or an element of a given set.
    a. Thing
    b. Function0
    c. Undefined
    d. Undefined

14. A _____ of a number is the product of that number with any integer.
    a. Multiple0
    b. Thing
    c. Undefined
    d. Undefined

15. In mathematics, the multiplicative inverse of a number x, denoted 1/x or x^{-1}, is the number which, when multiplied by x, yields 1. The multiplicative inverse of x is also called the _____ of x.
    a. Thing
    b. Reciprocal0
    c. Undefined
    d. Undefined

16. A _____ is the result of the addition of a set of numbers. The numbers may be natural numbers, complex numbers, matrices, or still more complicated objects. An infinite _____ is a subtle procedure known as a series.
    a. Sum0
    b. Thing
    c. Undefined
    d. Undefined

17. In calculus, the _____ in differentiation is a method of finding the derivative of a function that is the sum of two other functions for which derivatives exist.
    a. Sum Rule0
    b. Thing
    c. Undefined
    d. Undefined

18. In mathematics, _____ expressions is used to reduce the expression into the lowest possible term.
    a. Thing
    b. Simplifying0
    c. Undefined
    d. Undefined

Chapter 5. Integration and Its Applications

19. Fixed costs are expenses whose total does not change in proportion to the activity of a business. Unit fixed costs decline with volume following a retangular hyperbola as the volume of production. Variable costs by contrast change in relation to the activity of a business such as sales or production volume. Along with variable costs, fixed costs make up one of the two components of total cost. In the most simple production function total cost is equal to fixed costs plus variable costs. In accounting terminology, fixed costs will broadly include all costs which are not included in cost of goods sold, and variable costs are those captured in costs of goods sold. The implicit assumption required to make the equivalence between the accounting and economics terminology is that the accounting period is equal to the period in which fixed costs do not vary in relation to production. In practice, this equivalence does not always hold and depending on the period under consideration by management, some overhead expenses can be adjusted by management, and the specific allocation of each expense to each category will be decided under cost accounting. In business planning and management accounting, usage of the terms fixed costs, variable costs and others will often differ from usage in economics, and may depend on the intended use. For example, costs may be segregated into per unit costs fixed costs per period, and variable costs as a proportion of revenue. Capital expenditures will usually be allocated separately, and depending on the purpose, a portion may be regularly allocated to expenses as depreciation and amortization and seen as a _____ per period, or the entire amount may be considered upfront fixed costs.
    a. Fixed cost0
    b. Thing
    c. Undefined
    d. Undefined

20. _____ are expenses whose total does not change in proportion to the activity of a business, within the relevant time period or scale of production
    a. Fixed costs0
    b. Thing
    c. Undefined
    d. Undefined

21. _____ is the change in total cost that arises when the quantity produced changes by one unit.
    a. Thing
    b. Marginal cost0
    c. Undefined
    d. Undefined

22. A _____ is a special kind of ratio, indicating a relationship between two measurements with different units, such as miles to gallons or cents to pounds.
    a. Rate0
    b. Thing
    c. Undefined
    d. Undefined

23. In mathematics, the concept of a _____ tries to capture the intuitive idea of a geometrical one-dimensional and continuous object. A simple example is the circle.
    a. Curve0
    b. Thing
    c. Undefined
    d. Undefined

24. In mathematics, _____ are the intuitive idea of a geometrical one-dimensional and continuous object.
    a. Curves0
    b. Thing
    c. Undefined
    d. Undefined

25. In linear algebra, the _____ of an n-by-n square matrix A is defined to be the sum of the elements on the main diagonal of A,
    a. Trace0
    b. Thing
    c. Undefined
    d. Undefined

Chapter 5. Integration and Its Applications

26. A _____ function is a function for which, intuitively, small changes in the input result in small changes in the output.
   a. Continuous0
   b. Event
   c. Undefined
   d. Undefined

27. In mathematics, a _____ is an expression that is constructed from one or more variables and constants, using only the operations of addition, subtraction, multiplication, and constant positive whole number exponents. is a _____. Note in particular that division by an expression containing a variable is not in general allowed in polynomials. [1]
   a. Polynomial0
   b. Thing
   c. Undefined
   d. Undefined

28. _____ is a branch of mathematics concerning the study of structure, relation and quantity.
   a. Concept
   b. Algebra0
   c. Undefined
   d. Undefined

29. _____, from Latin meaning "to make progress", is defined in two different ways. Pure economic _____ is the increase in wealth that an investor has from making an investment, taking into consideration all costs associated with that investment including the opportunity cost of capital.
   a. Thing
   b. Profit0
   c. Undefined
   d. Undefined

30. _____ of an object is its speed in a particular direction.
   a. Velocity0
   b. Thing
   c. Undefined
   d. Undefined

31. _____ is often used to describe the measurement of the steepness, incline, gradient, or grade of a straight line. The _____ is defined as the ratio of the "rise" divided by the "run" between two points on a line, or in other words, the ratio of the altitude change to the horizontal distance between any two points on the line.
   a. Thing
   b. Slope0
   c. Undefined
   d. Undefined

32. _____ is a business term for the amount of money that a company receives from its activities in a given period, mostly from sales of products and/or services to customers
   a. Revenue0
   b. Thing
   c. Undefined
   d. Undefined

33. The _____ of measurement are a globally standardized and modernized form of the metric system.
   a. Units0
   b. Thing
   c. Undefined
   d. Undefined

34. _____ is the transport of people on a trip/journey or the process or time involved in a person or object moving from one location to another.
   a. Thing
   b. Travel0
   c. Undefined
   d. Undefined

35. _____ are a measure of time.

a. Minutes0   b. Thing
c. Undefined   d. Undefined

36. _____ is a temperature scale named after the German physicist Daniel Gabriel _____ , who proposed it in 1724.
   a. Fahrenheit0   b. Thing
   c. Undefined   d. Undefined

37. In mathematics, there are several meanings of _____ depending on the subject.
   a. Thing   b. Degree0
   c. Undefined   d. Undefined

38. _____ is a physical property of a system that underlies the common notions of hot and cold; something that is hotter has the greater _____.
   a. Temperature0   b. Thing
   c. Undefined   d. Undefined

39. _____ is a kind of property which exists as magnitude or multitude. It is among the basic classes of things along with quality, substance, change, and relation.
   a. Thing   b. Amount0
   c. Undefined   d. Undefined

40. In mathematics, a _____ is a demonstration that, assuming certain axioms, some statement is necessarily true.
   a. Proof0   b. Thing
   c. Undefined   d. Undefined

41. In mathematics, _____ growth occurs when the growth rate of a function is always proportional to the function's current size.
   a. Exponential0   b. Thing
   c. Undefined   d. Undefined

42. _____ is one of the most important functions in mathematics. A function commonly used to study growth and decay
   a. Exponential function0   b. Thing
   c. Undefined   d. Undefined

43. Initial objects are also called _____, and terminal objects are also called final.
   a. Coterminal0   b. Thing
   c. Undefined   d. Undefined

44. In epidemiology, an _____ is a disease that appears as new cases in a given human population, during a given period, at a rate that substantially exceeds with is "expected," based on recent experience.
   a. Thing   b. Epidemic0
   c. Undefined   d. Undefined

45. The _____ is the total number of human beings alive on the planet Earth at a given time.

68 *Chapter 5. Integration and Its Applications*

    a. Thing
    c. Undefined
    b. World population0
    d. Undefined

46. In sociology and biology a _____ is the collection of people or organisms of a particular species living in a given geographic area or space, usually measured by a census.
    a. Thing
    c. Undefined
    b. Population0
    d. Undefined

47. In mathematics a _____ is a function which defines a distance between elements of a set.
    a. Thing
    c. Undefined
    b. Metric0
    d. Undefined

48. _____ is the addition of a set of numbers; the result is their sum. The "numbers" to be summed may be natural numbers, complex numbers, matrices, or still more complicated objects. An infinite sum is a subtle procedure known as a series.
    a. Thing
    c. Undefined
    b. Summation0
    d. Undefined

49. The _____, the average in everyday English, which is also called the arithmetic _____ (and is distinguished from the geometric _____ or harmonic _____). The average is also called the sample _____. The expected value of a random variable, which is also called the population _____.
    a. Thing
    c. Undefined
    b. Mean0
    d. Undefined

50. _____ is the logarithm to the base e, where e is an irrational constant approximately equal to 2.718281828459.
    a. Thing
    c. Undefined
    b. Natural logarithm0
    d. Undefined

51. In mathematics, a _____ of a number x is the exponent y of the power by such that $x = b^y$. The value used for the base b must be neither 0 nor 1, nor a root of 1 in the case of the extension to complex numbers, and is typically 10, e, or 2.
    a. Logarithm0
    c. Undefined
    b. Thing
    d. Undefined

52. _____ is a list of goods and materials, or those goods and materials themselves, held available in stock by a business
    a. Inventory0
    c. Undefined
    b. Thing
    d. Undefined

53. A _____ is a three-dimensional solid object bounded by six square faces, facets, or sides, with three meeting at each vertex.
    a. Cube0
    c. Undefined
    b. Thing
    d. Undefined

54. _____ or investing is a term with several closely-related meanings in business management, finance and economics, related to saving or deferring consumption.

Chapter 5. Integration and Its Applications

a. Investment0
c. Undefined
b. Thing
d. Undefined

55. _____ is an extension of the concept of a sum.
    a. Definite integral0
    c. Undefined
    b. Thing
    d. Undefined

56. In mathematics, a _____ is a statement that can be proved on the basis of explicitly stated or previously agreed assumptions.
    a. Theorem0
    c. Undefined
    b. Thing
    d. Undefined

57. _____ is a mathematical subject that includes the study of limits, derivatives, integrals, and power series and constitutes a major part of modern university curriculum.
    a. Calculus0
    c. Undefined
    b. Thing
    d. Undefined

58. In number theory, the _____ of arithmetic (or unique factorization theorem) states that every natural number greater than 1 can be written as a unique product of prime numbers.
    a. Concept
    c. Undefined
    b. Fundamental theorem0
    d. Undefined

59. In geometry, a _____ is defined as a quadrilateral where all four of its angles are right angles.
    a. Rectangle0
    c. Undefined
    b. Thing
    d. Undefined

60. _____ is a set, with some particular properties and usually some additional structure, such as the operations of addition or multiplication, for instance.
    a. Thing
    c. Undefined
    b. Space0
    d. Undefined

61. In plane geometry, a _____ is a polygon with four equal sides, four right angles, and parallel opposite sides. In algebra, the _____ of a number is that number multiplied by itself.
    a. Square0
    c. Undefined
    b. Thing
    d. Undefined

62. In mathematics, a matrix can be thought of as each row or _____ being a vector. Hence, a space formed by row vectors or _____ vectors are said to be a row space or a _____ space.
    a. Column0
    c. Undefined
    b. Concept
    d. Undefined

63. The _____ integers are all the integers from zero on upwards.
    a. Thing
    c. Undefined
    b. Nonnegative0
    d. Undefined

64. _____ is the state of being greater than any finite number, however large.

Chapter 5. Integration and Its Applications

    a. Thing
    c. Undefined
    b. Infinity0
    d. Undefined

65. _____ is a method for approximating the values of integrals.
    a. Thing
    c. Undefined
    b. Riemann sum0
    d. Undefined

66. _____ was a German mathematician who made important contributions to analysis and differential geometry, some of them paving the way for the later development of general relativity.
    a. Georg Bernhard Riemann0
    c. Undefined
    b. Person
    d. Undefined

67. A _____ is a function for which, intuitively, small changes in the input result in small changes in the output.
    a. Event
    c. Undefined
    b. Continuous function0
    d. Undefined

68. In elementary algebra, an _____ is a set that contains every real number between two indicated numbers and may contain the two numbers themselves.
    a. Interval0
    c. Undefined
    b. Thing
    d. Undefined

69. A _____ is a simplified and structured visual representation of concepts, ideas, constructions, relations, statistical data, anatomy etc used in all aspects of human activities to visualize and clarify the topic.
    a. Diagram0
    c. Undefined
    b. Thing
    d. Undefined

70. Mathematical _____ is used to represent ideas.
    a. Notation0
    c. Undefined
    b. Thing
    d. Undefined

71. An _____ is a combination of numbers, operators, grouping symbols and/or free variables and bound variables arranged in a meaningful way which can be evaluated..
    a. Expression0
    c. Undefined
    b. Thing
    d. Undefined

72. The _____ (symbol _____) and the millibar (symbol mbar, also mb) are units of pressure.
    a. Bar0
    c. Undefined
    b. Thing
    d. Undefined

73. In mathematics, an _____, mean, or central tendency of a data set refers to a measure of the "middle" or "expected" value of the data set.
    a. Average0
    c. Undefined
    b. Concept
    d. Undefined

74. In geometry, the _____ of an object is a point in some sense in the middle of the object.

a. Thing
b. Center0
c. Undefined
d. Undefined

75. In classical geometry, a _____ of a circle or sphere is any line segment from its center to its boundary. By extension, the _____ of a circle or sphere is the length of any such segment. The _____ is half the diameter. In science and engineering the term _____ of curvature is commonly used as a synonym for _____.
a. Radius0
b. Thing
c. Undefined
d. Undefined

76. _____ are economic entities that give rise to future economic benefit and is controlled by the entity as a result of past transaction or other events
a. Thing
b. Asset0
c. Undefined
d. Undefined

77. _____ is the flow of blood in the cardiovascular system.
a. Thing
b. Blood flow0
c. Undefined
d. Undefined

78. _____ of a single or multiple future payments is the nominal amounts of money to change hands at some future date, discounted to account for the time value of money, and other factors such as investment risk.
a. Present value0
b. Thing
c. Undefined
d. Undefined

79. _____ is the fee paid on borrowed money.
a. Interest0
b. Thing
c. Undefined
d. Undefined

80. An _____ is the fee paid on borrow money.
a. Interest rate0
b. Concept
c. Undefined
d. Undefined

81. In mathematics, a _____ is a mathematical statement which appears likely to be true, but has not been formally proven to be true under the rules of mathematical logic.
a. Conjecture0
b. Concept
c. Undefined
d. Undefined

82. Compass and straightedge or ruler-and-compass _____ is the _____ of lengths or angles using only an idealized ruler and compass.
a. Construction0
b. Thing
c. Undefined
d. Undefined

83. The plus and _____ signs are mathematical symbols used to represent the notions of positive and negative as well as the operations of addition and subtraction.
a. Minus0
b. Thing
c. Undefined
d. Undefined

Chapter 5. Integration and Its Applications

84. In mathematics, the _____ of two sets A and B is the set that contains all elements of A that also belong to B (or equivalently, all elements of B that also belong to A), but no other elements.
   a. Thing
   b. Intersection0
   c. Undefined
   d. Undefined

85. In mathematical analysis and related areas of mathematics, a set is called _____, if it is, in a certain sense, of finite size.
   a. Bounded0
   b. Thing
   c. Undefined
   d. Undefined

86. Acid _____ ratio measures the ability of a company to use its near cash or quick assets to immediately extinguish its current liabilities.
   a. Thing
   b. Test0
   c. Undefined
   d. Undefined

87. A _____ is one of the basic shapes of geometry: a polygon with three vertices and three sides which are straight line segments.
   a. Thing
   b. Triangle0
   c. Undefined
   d. Undefined

88. In Euclidean geometry, a _____ is the set of all points in a plane at a fixed distance, called the radius, from a given point, the center.
   a. Thing
   b. Circle0
   c. Undefined
   d. Undefined

89. The easiest _____ prime numbers resides in the use of the Sieve of Eratosthenes, an algorithm that discovers all prime numbers to a specified integer.
   a. Thing
   b. Method for finding0
   c. Undefined
   d. Undefined

90. _____ interest refers to the fact that whenever interest is calculated, it is based not only on the original principal, but also on any unpaid interest that has been added to the principal.
   a. Thing
   b. Compound0
   c. Undefined
   d. Undefined

91. _____ refers to the fact that whenever interest is calculated, it is based not only on the original principal, but also on any unpaid interest that has been added to the principal. The more frequently interest is compounded, the faster the balance grows.
   a. Concept
   b. Compound interest0
   c. Undefined
   d. Undefined

92. In mathematics, the _____ is a conic section generated by the intersection of a right circular conical surface and a plane parallel to a generating straight line of that surface. It can also be defined as locus of points in a plane which are equidistant from a given point.

Chapter 5. Integration and Its Applications

a. Parabola0
b. Thing
c. Undefined
d. Undefined

93. In topology and related areas of mathematics a _____ or Moore-Smith sequence is a generalization of a sequence, intended to unify the various notions of limit and generalize them to arbitrary topological spaces.
a. Net0
b. Thing
c. Undefined
d. Undefined

94. _____ is a synonym for information.
a. Thing
b. Data0
c. Undefined
d. Undefined

95. The word _____ comes from the Latin word linearis, which means created by lines.
a. Linear0
b. Thing
c. Undefined
d. Undefined

96. _____ is a regression method that models the relationship between a dependent variable Y, independent variables Xp, and a random term à.
a. Thing
b. Linear regression0
c. Undefined
d. Undefined

97. In mathematics, a _____ is the result of multiplying, or an expression that identifies factors to be multiplied.
a. Thing
b. Product0
c. Undefined
d. Undefined

98. A _____ is an individual or household that purchases and uses goods and services generated within the economy.
a. Consumer0
b. Thing
c. Undefined
d. Undefined

99. In business, particularly accounting, a _____ is the time intervals that the accounts, statement, payments, or other calculations cover.
a. Thing
b. Period0
c. Undefined
d. Undefined

100. A _____ is a function that assigns a number to subsets of a given set.
a. Thing
b. Measure0
c. Undefined
d. Undefined

101. In economics, supply and _____ describe market relations between prospective sellers and buyers of a good.
a. Thing
b. Demand0
c. Undefined
d. Undefined

102. _____ can be defined as the graph depicting the relationship between the price of a certain commodity, and the amount of it that consumers are willing and able to purchase at that given price demand.

a. Thing
b. Demand curve0
c. Undefined
d. Undefined

103. In economics, _____ describe market relations between prospective sellers and buyers of a good.
a. Supply and demand0
b. Thing
c. Undefined
d. Undefined

104. The word _____ is used in a variety of ways in mathematics.
a. Thing
b. Index0
c. Undefined
d. Undefined

105. In mathematical analysis, _____ are objects which generalize functions and probability distributions.
a. Thing
b. Distribution0
c. Undefined
d. Undefined

106. _____ is a special mathematical relationship between two quantities.Two quantities are called proportional if they vary in such a way that one of the quantities is a constant multiple of the other, or equivalently if they have a constant ratio.
a. Proportionality0
b. Thing
c. Undefined
d. Undefined

107. _____ (Groups, Algorithms and Programming) is a computer algebra system for computational discrete algebra with particular emphasis on, but not restricted to, computational group theory.
a. Gap0
b. Thing
c. Undefined
d. Undefined

108. Two mathematical objects are equal if and only if they are precisely the same in every way. This defines a binary relation, _____, denoted by the sign of _____ "=" in such a way that the statement "x = y" means that x and y are equal.
a. Equality0
b. Thing
c. Undefined
d. Undefined

109. In mathematics, an _____ is a statement about the relative size or order of two objects.
a. Thing
b. Inequality0
c. Undefined
d. Undefined

110. In mathematics, an inequality is a statement about the relative size or order of two objects. For example 14 > 10, or 14 is _____ 10.
a. Thing
b. Greater than0
c. Undefined
d. Undefined

111. _____ is the process of reducing the number of significant digits in a number.
a. Rounding0
b. Concept
c. Undefined
d. Undefined

112. In calculus, the _____ is a formula for the derivative of the composite of two functions.

Chapter 5. Integration and Its Applications

a. Concept
c. Undefined
b. Chain rule0
d. Undefined

113. In mathematics, the _____ of a function is the set of all "output" values produced by that function. Given a function $f : A \rightarrow B$, the _____ of f, is defined to be the set $\{x \in B : x = f(a)$ for some $a \in A\}$.
a. Thing
c. Undefined
b. Range0
d. Undefined

114. _____ is a tool for finding antiderivatives and integrals. Using the fundamental theorem of calculus often requires finding an antiderivative. For this and other reasons, this rule is a relatively important tool for mathematicians. It is the counterpart to the chain rule of differentiation.
a. Integration by substitution0
c. Undefined
b. Thing
d. Undefined

115. In mathematics, a _____ is the end result of a division problem. It can also be expressed as the number of times the divisor divides into the dividend.
a. Thing
c. Undefined
b. Quotient0
d. Undefined

116. A _____ is traditionally an infinitesimally small change in a variable.
a. Thing
c. Undefined
b. Differential0
d. Undefined

117. A _____ is a numeral used to indicate a count. The most common use of the word today is to name the part of a fraction that tells the number or count of equal parts.
a. Thing
c. Undefined
b. Numerator0
d. Undefined

118. A _____ is the part of a fraction that tells how many equal parts make up a whole, and which is used in the name of the fraction: "halves", "thirds", "fourths" or "quarters", "fifths" and so on.
a. Concept
c. Undefined
b. Denominator0
d. Undefined

119. _____ is the estimation of a physical quantity such as distance, energy, temperature, or time.
a. Thing
c. Undefined
b. Measurement0
d. Undefined

120. _____ traditionally refers to the statistical process of determining comparable scores on different forms of an exam
a. Equating0
c. Undefined
b. Thing
d. Undefined

121. _____ is a mathematical operation, written a^n, involving two numbers, the base a and the exponent n.
a. Exponentiating0
c. Undefined
b. Thing
d. Undefined

122. _____ is a mathematical operation, written a^n, involving two numbers, the base a and the exponent n.
a. Exponentiation0
b. Thing
c. Undefined
d. Undefined

123. The _____ is used to discard one of the variables in an equation, only to replace it with the actual value when solving multiple equations.
a. Thing
b. Substitution method0
c. Undefined
d. Undefined

124. In mathematics, science including computer science, linguistics and engineering, an _____ is, generally speaking, an independent variable or input to a function.
a. Argument0
b. Thing
c. Undefined
d. Undefined

125. In mathematics, the _____ (or modulus) of a real number is its numerical value without regard to its sign.
a. Absolute value0
b. Thing
c. Undefined
d. Undefined

126. _____, either of the curved-bracket punctuation marks that together make a set of _____
a. Parentheses0
b. Thing
c. Undefined
d. Undefined

127. _____ is the extra revenue that an additional unit of product will bring a firm. It can also be described as the change in total revenue/change in number of units sold.
a. Thing
b. Marginal revenue0
c. Undefined
d. Undefined

128. The population _____ is the total number of human beings alive on the planet Earth at a given time.
a. Of the world0
b. Thing
c. Undefined
d. Undefined

129. A _____ is a mathematical equation for an unknown function of one or several variables which relates the values of the function itself and of its derivatives of various orders.
a. Thing
b. Differential equation0
c. Undefined
d. Undefined

Chapter 6. Integration Techniques and Differential Equations

1. _____ is a process of combining or accumulating. It may also refer to:
   a. Integration0
   b. Thing
   c. Undefined
   d. Undefined

2. _____, a field in mathematics, is the study of how functions change when their inputs change. The primary object of study in _____ is the derivative.
   a. Thing
   b. Differential calculus0
   c. Undefined
   d. Undefined

3. _____ element of an element x with respect to a binary operation * with identity element e is an element y such that x * y = y * x = e. In particular,
   a. Thing
   b. Inverse0
   c. Undefined
   d. Undefined

4. In mathematics, a _____ is the result of multiplying, or an expression that identifies factors to be multiplied.
   a. Product0
   b. Thing
   c. Undefined
   d. Undefined

5. In mathematics, a _____ is the end result of a division problem. It can also be expressed as the number of times the divisor divides into the dividend.
   a. Thing
   b. Quotient0
   c. Undefined
   d. Undefined

6. The _____ is a method of finding the derivative of a function that is the quotient of two other functions for which derivatives exist.
   a. Quotient rule0
   b. Thing
   c. Undefined
   d. Undefined

7. An _____ is a combination of numbers, operators, grouping symbols and/or free variables and bound variables arranged in a meaningful way which can be evaluated..
   a. Thing
   b. Expression0
   c. Undefined
   d. Undefined

8. The _____ governs the differentiation of products of differentiable functions.
   a. Thing
   b. Product rule0
   c. Undefined
   d. Undefined

9. The _____ is a measurement of how a function changes when the values of its inputs change.
   a. Derivative0
   b. Thing
   c. Undefined
   d. Undefined

10. The mathematical concept of a _____ expresses the intuitive idea of deterministic dependence between two quantities, one of which is viewed as primary and the other as secondary. A _____ then is a way to associate a unique output for each input of a specified type, for example, a real number or an element of a given set.
    a. Function0
    b. Thing
    c. Undefined
    d. Undefined

Chapter 6. Integration Techniques and Differential Equations

11. Mathematical _____ is used to represent ideas.
    a. Thing
    b. Notation0
    c. Undefined
    d. Undefined

12. The _____ of a function is an extension of the concept of a sum, and are identified or found through the use of integration.
    a. Thing
    b. Integral0
    c. Undefined
    d. Undefined

13. A _____ is traditionally an infinitesimally small change in a variable.
    a. Differential0
    b. Thing
    c. Undefined
    d. Undefined

14. A _____ is a negotiable instrument instructing a financial institution to pay a specific amount of a specific currency from a specific demand account held in the maker/depositor's name with that institution. Both the maker and payee may be natural persons or legal entities.
    a. Thing
    b. Check0
    c. Undefined
    d. Undefined

15. _____ are any documents that aim to streamline particular processes according to a set routine.
    a. Thing
    b. Guidelines0
    c. Undefined
    d. Undefined

16. A _____ function is a function for which, intuitively, small changes in the input result in small changes in the output.
    a. Continuous0
    b. Event
    c. Undefined
    d. Undefined

17. A _____ is a special kind of ratio, indicating a relationship between two measurements with different units, such as miles to gallons or cents to pounds.
    a. Rate0
    b. Thing
    c. Undefined
    d. Undefined

18. _____ is the fee paid on borrowed money.
    a. Thing
    b. Interest0
    c. Undefined
    d. Undefined

19. _____ of a single or multiple future payments is the nominal amounts of money to change hands at some future date, discounted to account for the time value of money, and other factors such as investment risk.
    a. Present value0
    b. Thing
    c. Undefined
    d. Undefined

20. An _____ is the fee paid on borrow money.
    a. Interest rate0
    b. Concept
    c. Undefined
    d. Undefined

Chapter 6. Integration Techniques and Differential Equations

21. In mathematics, the concept of a _____ tries to capture the intuitive idea of a geometrical one-dimensional and continuous object. A simple example is the circle.
    a. Curve0
    b. Thing
    c. Undefined
    d. Undefined

22. In mathematics and the mathematical sciences, a _____ is a fixed, but possibly unspecified, value. This is in contrast to a variable, which is not fixed.
    a. Thing
    b. Constant0
    c. Undefined
    d. Undefined

23. In calculus, the indefinite integral of a given function i.e. the set of all antiderivatives of the function is always written with a constant, the _____.
    a. Constant of integration0
    b. Thing
    c. Undefined
    d. Undefined

24. _____ is a business term for the amount of money that a company receives from its activities in a given period, mostly from sales of products and/or services to customers
    a. Thing
    b. Revenue0
    c. Undefined
    d. Undefined

25. _____ is a kind of property which exists as magnitude or multitude. It is among the basic classes of things along with quality, substance, change, and relation.
    a. Thing
    b. Amount0
    c. Undefined
    d. Undefined

26. Fixed costs are expenses whose total does not change in proportion to the activity of a business. Unit fixed costs decline with volume following a retangular hyperbola as the volume of production. Variable costs by contrast change in relation to the activity of a business such as sales or production volume. Along with variable costs, fixed costs make up one of the two components of total cost. In the most simple production function total cost is equal to fixed costs plus variable costs. In accounting terminology, fixed costs will broadly include all costs which are not included in cost of goods sold, and variable costs are those captured in costs of goods sold. The implicit assumption required to make the equivalence between the accounting and economics terminology is that the accounting period is equal to the period in which fixed costs do not vary in relation to production. In practice, this equivalence does not always hold and depending on the period under consideration by management, some overhead expenses can be adjusted by management, and the specific allocation of each expense to each category will be decided under cost accounting. In business planning and management accounting, usage of the terms fixed costs, variable costs and others will often differ from usage in economics, and may depend on the intended use. For example, costs may be segregated into per unit costs fixed costs per period, and variable costs as a proportion of revenue. Capital expenditures will usually be allocated separately, and depending on the purpose, a portion may be regularly allocated to expenses as depreciation and amortization and seen as a _____ per period, or the entire amount may be considered upfront fixed costs.
    a. Thing
    b. Fixed cost0
    c. Undefined
    d. Undefined

27. _____ are expenses whose total does not change in proportion to the activity of a business, within the relevant time period or scale of production

Chapter 6. Integration Techniques and Differential Equations

a. Thing
b. Fixed costs0
c. Undefined
d. Undefined

28. In sociology and biology a _____ is the collection of people or organisms of a particular species living in a given geographic area or space, usually measured by a census.
 a. Population0
 b. Thing
 c. Undefined
 d. Undefined

29. The deductive-nomological model is a formalized view of scientific _____ in natural language.
 a. Explanation0
 b. Thing
 c. Undefined
 d. Undefined

30. _____ is the design, analysis, and/or construction of works for practical purposes.
 a. Engineering0
 b. Thing
 c. Undefined
 d. Undefined

31. In statistics the _____ of an event i is the number n_i of times the event occurred in the experiment or the study. These frequencies are often graphically represented in histograms.
 a. Frequency0
 b. Concept
 c. Undefined
 d. Undefined

32. In mathematics, _____ refers to the rewriting of an expression into a simpler form.
 a. Thing
 b. Reduction0
 c. Undefined
 d. Undefined

33. In mathematics, _____ is the decomposition of an object into a product of other objects, or factors, which when multiplied together give the original.
 a. Thing
 b. Factoring0
 c. Undefined
 d. Undefined

34. _____ has many meanings, most of which simply .
 a. Thing
 b. Power0
 c. Undefined
 d. Undefined

35. _____ is an extension of the concept of a sum.
 a. Thing
 b. Definite integral0
 c. Undefined
 d. Undefined

36. A _____ is a numeral used to indicate a count. The most common use of the word today is to name the part of a fraction that tells the number or count of equal parts.
 a. Numerator0
 b. Thing
 c. Undefined
 d. Undefined

37. A _____ is the result of the addition of a set of numbers. The numbers may be natural numbers, complex numbers, matrices, or still more complicated objects. An infinite _____ is a subtle procedure known as a series.

Chapter 6. Integration Techniques and Differential Equations 81

   a. Thing   b. Sum0
   c. Undefined   d. Undefined

38. _____ is the change in total cost that arises when the quantity produced changes by one unit.
   a. Marginal cost0   b. Thing
   c. Undefined   d. Undefined

39. In geometry, the _____ of an object is a point in some sense in the middle of the object.
   a. Thing   b. Center0
   c. Undefined   d. Undefined

40. In mathematics, an _____, mean, or central tendency of a data set refers to a measure of the "middle" or "expected" value of the data set.
   a. Concept   b. Average0
   c. Undefined   d. Undefined

41. In business, particularly accounting, a _____ is the time intervals that the accounts, statement, payments, or other calculations cover.
   a. Thing   b. Period0
   c. Undefined   d. Undefined

42. _____ is the state of being greater than any finite number, however large.
   a. Thing   b. Infinity0
   c. Undefined   d. Undefined

43. The _____, the average in everyday English, which is also called the arithmetic _____ (and is distinguished from the geometric _____ or harmonic _____). The average is also called the sample _____. The expected value of a random variable, which is also called the population _____.
   a. Thing   b. Mean0
   c. Undefined   d. Undefined

44. A _____ is a one-dimensional picture in which the integers are shown as specially-marked points evenly spaced on a line.
   a. Thing   b. Number line0
   c. Undefined   d. Undefined

45. In mathematics, the multiplicative inverse of a number x, denoted $1/x$ or x^{-1}, is the number which, when multiplied by x, yields 1. The multiplicative inverse of x is also called the _____ of x.
   a. Reciprocal0   b. Thing
   c. Undefined   d. Undefined

46. An _____ is the limit of a definite integral, as an endpoint of the interval of integration approaches either a specified real number or ‡ or − ‡ or, in some cases, as both endpoints approach limits.
   a. Improper integral0   b. Thing
   c. Undefined   d. Undefined

Chapter 6. Integration Techniques and Differential Equations

47. In mathematics, a set is called _____ if there is a bijection between the set and some set of the form {1, 2, ..., n} where n is a natural number.
    a. Finite0
    b. Thing
    c. Undefined
    d. Undefined

48. In elementary algebra, an _____ is a set that contains every real number between two indicated numbers and may contain the two numbers themselves.
    a. Thing
    b. Interval0
    c. Undefined
    d. Undefined

49. In mathematics, _____ describes an entity with a limit.
    a. Convergent0
    b. Thing
    c. Undefined
    d. Undefined

50. In mathematics, a _____ series is an infinite series that is not convergent, meaning that the infinite sequence of the partial sums of the series does not have a limit.
    a. Thing
    b. Divergent0
    c. Undefined
    d. Undefined

51. _____ are rectangular tables (or grids) of information, often financial information.
    a. Spreadsheets0
    b. Thing
    c. Undefined
    d. Undefined

52. In mathematics, a matrix can be thought of as each row or _____ being a vector. Hence, a space formed by row vectors or _____ vectors are said to be a row space or a _____ space.
    a. Column0
    b. Concept
    c. Undefined
    d. Undefined

53. _____ is a transfer of money or property donated to an institution, with the stipulation that it be invested, and the principal remain intact.
    a. Thing
    b. Endowment0
    c. Undefined
    d. Undefined

54. _____ is a function that extends the concept of an ordinary sum
    a. Thing
    b. Integrand0
    c. Undefined
    d. Undefined

55. In mathematics, _____ is an elementary arithmetic operation. When one of the numbers is a whole number, _____ is the repeated sum of the other number.
    a. Multiplication0
    b. Thing
    c. Undefined
    d. Undefined

56. The _____ integers are all the integers from zero on upwards.
    a. Nonnegative0
    b. Thing
    c. Undefined
    d. Undefined

Chapter 6. Integration Techniques and Differential Equations

57. _____ is the state of being greater than any finite real or natural number, however large.
   a. Infinite0
   b. Thing
   c. Undefined
   d. Undefined

58. _____ are economic entities that give rise to future economic benefit and is controlled by the entity as a result of past transaction or other events
   a. Asset0
   b. Thing
   c. Undefined
   d. Undefined

59. _____ is a special mathematical relationship between two quantities.Two quantities are called proportional if they vary in such a way that one of the quantities is a constant multiple of the other, or equivalently if they have a constant ratio.
   a. Thing
   b. Proportionality0
   c. Undefined
   d. Undefined

60. _____ are a measure of time.
   a. Minutes0
   b. Thing
   c. Undefined
   d. Undefined

61. _____ is electromagnetic radiation with a wavelength that is visible to the eye (visible _____) or, in a technical or scientific context, electromagnetic radiation of any wavelength.
   a. Light0
   b. Thing
   c. Undefined
   d. Undefined

62. _____, in economics and political economy, are the distributions or payments awarded to the various suppliers of the factors of production.
   a. Thing
   b. Returns0
   c. Undefined
   d. Undefined

63. Initial objects are also called _____, and terminal objects are also called final.
   a. Thing
   b. Coterminal0
   c. Undefined
   d. Undefined

64. _____ constitutes a broad family of algorithms for calculating the numerical value of a definite integral, and by extension, the term is also sometimes used to describe the numerical solution of differential equations.
   a. Numerical integration0
   b. Thing
   c. Undefined
   d. Undefined

65. _____ is a payment made by a company to its shareholders
   a. Thing
   b. Dividend0
   c. Undefined
   d. Undefined

66. _____ is change in population over time, and can be quantified as the change in the number of individuals in a population per unit time.

84 Chapter 6. Integration Techniques and Differential Equations

   a. Population growth0
   b. Thing
   c. Undefined
   d. Undefined

67. In geometry, a _____ is defined as a quadrilateral where all four of its angles are right angles.
   a. Rectangle0
   b. Thing
   c. Undefined
   d. Undefined

68. _____ is a method for approximating the values of integrals.
   a. Thing
   b. Riemann sum0
   c. Undefined
   d. Undefined

69. A _____ is a quadrilateral, which is defined as a shape with four sides, which has a pair of parallel sides.
   a. Trapezoid0
   b. Thing
   c. Undefined
   d. Undefined

70. _____ are external two-dimensional outlines, with the appearance or configuration of some thing - in contrast to the matter or content or substance of which it is composed.
   a. Shapes0
   b. Thing
   c. Undefined
   d. Undefined

71. _____ is a way of expressing a number as a fraction of 100 per cent meaning "per hundred".
   a. Percent0
   b. Thing
   c. Undefined
   d. Undefined

72. In the mathematical field of numerical analysis, the _____ in some data is the discrepancy between an exact value and some approximation to it.
   a. Approximation Error0
   b. Thing
   c. Undefined
   d. Undefined

73. In mathematics, the _____ (or modulus) of a real number is its numerical value without regard to its sign.
   a. Thing
   b. Absolute value0
   c. Undefined
   d. Undefined

74. In mathematics, there are several meanings of _____ depending on the subject.
   a. Thing
   b. Degree0
   c. Undefined
   d. Undefined

75. In mathematics, _____ are the intuitive idea of a geometrical one-dimensional and continuous object.
   a. Thing
   b. Curves0
   c. Undefined
   d. Undefined

76. In mathematics, the _____ is a conic section generated by the intersection of a right circular conical surface and a plane parallel to a generating straight line of that surface. It can also be defined as locus of points in a plane which are equidistant from a given point.

Chapter 6. Integration Techniques and Differential Equations

a. Thing
b. Parabola0
c. Undefined
d. Undefined

77. A _____ is a deliberate process for transforming one or more inputs into one or more results.
a. Calculation0
b. Thing
c. Undefined
d. Undefined

78. _____ was a British mathematician, inventor and eponym of Simpson's rule to approximate definite integrals.
a. Thomas Simpson0
b. Person
c. Undefined
d. Undefined

79. Acid _____ ratio measures the ability of a company to use its near cash or quick assets to immediately extinguish its current liabilities.
a. Thing
b. Test0
c. Undefined
d. Undefined

80. In mathematical analysis, _____ are objects which generalize functions and probability distributions.
a. Thing
b. Distribution0
c. Undefined
d. Undefined

81. _____ is a mathematical science pertaining to the collection, analysis, interpretation or explanation, and presentation of data. It is applicable to a wide variety of academic disciplines, from the physical and social sciences to the humanities.
a. Thing
b. Statistics0
c. Undefined
d. Undefined

82. An _____ is a score derived from one of several different standardized tests attempting to measure intelligence.
a. Intelligence Quotient0
b. Thing
c. Undefined
d. Undefined

83. In mathematics, _____ growth occurs when the growth rate of a function is always proportional to the function's current size.
a. Thing
b. Exponential0
c. Undefined
d. Undefined

84. In mathematics, a _____ of a number x is the exponent y of the power by such that $x = b^y$. The value used for the base b must be neither 0 nor 1, nor a root of 1 in the case of the extension to complex numbers, and is typically 10, e, or 2.
a. Thing
b. Logarithm0
c. Undefined
d. Undefined

85. _____ or investing is a term with several closely-related meanings in business management, finance and economics, related to saving or deferring consumption.
a. Thing
b. Investment0
c. Undefined
d. Undefined

Chapter 6. Integration Techniques and Differential Equations

86. A _____ fraction is a fraction in which the absolute value of the numerator is less than the denominator--hence, the absolute value of the fraction is less than 1.
   a. Proper0
   b. Thing
   c. Undefined
   d. Undefined

87. In mathematics, _____ expressions is used to reduce the expression into the lowest possible term.
   a. Thing
   b. Simplifying0
   c. Undefined
   d. Undefined

88. A _____ is a type of bridge that has been created since ancient times as early as 100 AD.
   a. Suspension bridge0
   b. Thing
   c. Undefined
   d. Undefined

89. A _____ is a symbolic representation denoting a quantity or expression. It often represents an "unknown" quantity that has the potential to change.
   a. Thing
   b. Variable0
   c. Undefined
   d. Undefined

90. A _____ is a mathematical equation for an unknown function of one or several variables which relates the values of the function itself and of its derivatives of various orders.
   a. Thing
   b. Differential equation0
   c. Undefined
   d. Undefined

91. _____ is a method for differentiating expressions involving exponentiation the power operation.
   a. Power rule0
   b. Thing
   c. Undefined
   d. Undefined

92. A _____ y_s of an ordinary differential equation is a solution that is tangent to every solution from the family of general solutions.
   a. Thing
   b. Singular solution0
   c. Undefined
   d. Undefined

93. In mathematics, the additive inverse, or _____ of a number n is the number that, when added to n, yields zero. The additive inverse of n is denoted −n. For example, 7 is −7, because 7 + (−7) = 0, and the additive inverse of −0.3 is 0.3, because −0.3 + 0.3 = 0.
   a. Opposite0
   b. Thing
   c. Undefined
   d. Undefined

94. In mathematics, the _____ of a number n is the number that, when added to n, yields zero. The _____ of n is denoted −n. For example, 7 is −7, because 7 + (−7) = 0, and the _____ of −0.3 is 0.3, because −0.3 + 0.3 = 0.
   a. Additive inverse0
   b. Thing
   c. Undefined
   d. Undefined

95. A _____ is a three-dimensional solid object bounded by six square faces, facets, or sides, with three meeting at each vertex.

Chapter 6. Integration Techniques and Differential Equations

    a. Thing
    c. Undefined
    b. Cube0
    d. Undefined

96. A _____ of a number is a number a such that $a^3 = x$.
    a. Thing
    c. Undefined
    b. Cube root0
    d. Undefined

97. In mathematics, a _____ of a complex-valued function f is a member x of the domain of f such that f(x) vanishes at x, that is, x : f (x) = 0.
    a. Thing
    c. Undefined
    b. Root0
    d. Undefined

98. In mathematics, in the field of differential equations, an initial value problem is a differential equation together with specified value, called the _____, of the unknown function at a given point in the domain of the solution.
    a. Thing
    c. Undefined
    b. Initial condition0
    d. Undefined

99. In Euclidean geometry, an _____ is a closed segment of a differentiable curve in the two-dimensional plane; for example, a circular _____ is a segment of a circle.
    a. Concept
    c. Undefined
    b. Arc0
    d. Undefined

100. The _____ (symbol _____) and the millibar (symbol mbar, also mb) are units of pressure.
    a. Bar0
    c. Undefined
    b. Thing
    d. Undefined

101. A _____ consists of one quarter of the coordinate plane.
    a. Quadrant0
    c. Undefined
    b. Thing
    d. Undefined

102. _____ is often used to describe the measurement of the steepness, incline, gradient, or grade of a straight line. The _____ is defined as the ratio of the "rise" divided by the "run" between two points on a line, or in other words, the ratio of the altitude change to the horizontal distance between any two points on the line.
    a. Thing
    c. Undefined
    b. Slope0
    d. Undefined

103. In plane geometry, a _____ is a polygon with four equal sides, four right angles, and parallel opposite sides. In algebra, the _____ of a number is that number multiplied by itself.
    a. Thing
    c. Undefined
    b. Square0
    d. Undefined

104. In mathematics, a _____ of a number x is a number r such that $r^2 = x$, or in words, a number r whose square (the result of multiplying the number by itself) is x.
    a. Square root0
    c. Undefined
    b. Thing
    d. Undefined

Chapter 6. Integration Techniques and Differential Equations

105. _____ is a mathematical operation, written a^n, involving two numbers, the base a and the exponent n.
 a. Exponentiating0
 b. Thing
 c. Undefined
 d. Undefined

106. In banking and accountancy, the outstanding _____ is the amount of money owned, or due, that remains in a deposit account or a loan account at a given date, after all past remittances, payments and withdrawal have been accounted for.
 a. Thing
 b. Balance0
 c. Undefined
 d. Undefined

107. A _____ is a graphical tool to qualitatively visualize, or aid in numerical approximation of, solutions to differential equations.
 a. Thing
 b. Slope field0
 c. Undefined
 d. Undefined

108. In mathematics, two quantities are called _____ if they vary in such a way that one of the quantities is a constant multiple of the other, or equivalently if they have a constant ratio.
 a. Thing
 b. Proportional0
 c. Undefined
 d. Undefined

109. In mathematics, a _____ function in the sense of algebraic geometry is an everywhere-defined, polynomial function on an algebraic variety V with values in the field K over which V is defined.
 a. Regular0
 b. Thing
 c. Undefined
 d. Undefined

110. _____ is the income from capital investment paid in a series of regular payments.
 a. Thing
 b. Annuity0
 c. Undefined
 d. Undefined

111. _____ is a physical property of a system that underlies the common notions of hot and cold; something that is hotter has the greater _____.
 a. Thing
 b. Temperature0
 c. Undefined
 d. Undefined

112. _____ is a temperature scale named after the German physicist Daniel Gabriel _____, who proposed it in 1724.
 a. Fahrenheit0
 b. Thing
 c. Undefined
 d. Undefined

113. In physics, _____ is an influence that may cause an object to accelerate. It may be experienced as a lift, a push, or a pull. The actual acceleration of the body is determined by the vector sum of all forces acting on it, known as net _____ or resultant _____.
 a. Force0
 b. Thing
 c. Undefined
 d. Undefined

114. _____ is the flow of blood in the cardiovascular system.

Chapter 6. Integration Techniques and Differential Equations

    a. Thing
    b. Blood flow0
    c. Undefined
    d. Undefined

115. The _____ of a solid object is the three-dimensional concept of how much space it occupies, often quantified numerically.
    a. Volume0
    b. Thing
    c. Undefined
    d. Undefined

116. _____ is the net action of matter particles or molecules, heat, momentum, or light whose end is to minimize a concentration gradient
    a. Diffusion0
    b. Thing
    c. Undefined
    d. Undefined

117. A _____ of a number is the product of that number with any integer.
    a. Thing
    b. Multiple0
    c. Undefined
    d. Undefined

118. _____ is a set, with some particular properties and usually some additional structure, such as the operations of addition or multiplication, for instance.
    a. Thing
    b. Space0
    c. Undefined
    d. Undefined

119. The _____ of measurement are a globally standardized and modernized form of the metric system.
    a. Units0
    b. Thing
    c. Undefined
    d. Undefined

120. _____ is the ability to hold, receive or absorb, or a measure thereof, similar to the concept of volume.
    a. Capacity0
    b. Concept
    c. Undefined
    d. Undefined

121. _____ usually refers to the biological _____ of a population level that can be supported for an organism, given the quantity of food, habitat, water and other life infrastructure present.
    a. Thing
    b. Carrying capacity0
    c. Undefined
    d. Undefined

122. In epidemiology, an _____ is a disease that appears as new cases in a given human population, during a given period, at a rate that substantially exceeds with is "expected," based on recent experience.
    a. Thing
    b. Epidemic0
    c. Undefined
    d. Undefined

123. A _____ models the S-curve of growth of some set P. The initial stage of growth is approximately exponential; then, as saturation begins, the growth slows, and at maturity, growth stops.
    a. Logistic function0
    b. Thing
    c. Undefined
    d. Undefined

124. _____ is a synonym for information.

Chapter 6. Integration Techniques and Differential Equations

    a. Data0   b. Thing
    c. Undefined   d. Undefined

125. The plus and _____ signs are mathematical symbols used to represent the notions of positive and negative as well as the operations of addition and subtraction.
    a. Thing   b. Minus0
    c. Undefined   d. Undefined

126. _____ the expected value of a random variable displays the average or central value of the variable. It is a summary value of the distribution of the variable.
    a. Determining0   b. Thing
    c. Undefined   d. Undefined

127. In mathematics, a _____ is a two-dimensional manifold or surface that is perfectly flat.
    a. Thing   b. Plane0
    c. Undefined   d. Undefined

128. _____ refers to all non-domesticated plants, animals, and other organisms.
    a. Wildlife0   b. Thing
    c. Undefined   d. Undefined

129. _____ Any process by which a specified characteristic usually amplitude of the output of a device is prevented from exceeding a predetermined value.
    a. Limiting0   b. Thing
    c. Undefined   d. Undefined

130. _____ named after Benjamin Gompertz, is a type of mathematical model for a time series, where growth is slowest at the start and end of a time period.
    a. Gompertz curve0   b. Thing
    c. Undefined   d. Undefined

131. In geometry, a _____ (Greek words diairo = divide and metro = measure) of a circle is any straight line segment that passes through the centre and whose endpoints are on the circular boundary, or, in more modern usage, the length of such a line segment. When using the word in the more modern sense, one speaks of the _____ rather than a _____, because all diameters of a circle have the same length. This length is twice the radius. The _____ of a circle is also the longest chord that the circle has.
    a. Diameter0   b. Thing
    c. Undefined   d. Undefined

132. _____ are waste types containing radioactive chemical elements that do not have a practical purpose.
    a. Radioactive waste0   b. Thing
    c. Undefined   d. Undefined

133. U.S. liquid _____ is legally defined as 231 cubic inches, and is equal to 3.785411784 litres or abotu 0.13368 cubic feet. This is the most common definition of a _____. The U.S. fluid ounce is defined as 1/128 of a U.S. _____.

Chapter 6. Integration Techniques and Differential Equations

    a. Thing
    b. Gallon0
    c. Undefined
    d. Undefined

134. _____, in law and economics, is a form of risk management primarily used to hedge against the risk of a contingent loss.
    a. Insurance0
    b. Thing
    c. Undefined
    d. Undefined

135. Sir Isaac _____, was an English physicist, mathematician, astronomer, natural philosopher, and alchemist, regarded by many as the greatest figure in the history of science
    a. Person
    b. Newton0
    c. Undefined
    d. Undefined

136. _____ is the general term that is used to describe physical artifacts of a technology.
    a. Hardware0
    b. Thing
    c. Undefined
    d. Undefined

137. _____ is the level of functional and/or metabolic efficiency of an organism at both the micro level.
    a. Health0
    b. Thing
    c. Undefined
    d. Undefined

138. In regression analysis, _____, also known as ordinary _____ analysis is a method for linear regression that determines the values of unknown quantities in a statistical model by minimizing the sum of the residuals difference between the predicted and observed values squared.
    a. Least squares0
    b. Thing
    c. Undefined
    d. Undefined

Chapter 7. Calculus of Several Variables

1. A _____ is a symbolic representation denoting a quantity or expression. It often represents an "unknown" quantity that has the potential to change.
   a. Thing
   b. Variable0
   c. Undefined
   d. Undefined

2. An _____ is a collection of two not necessarily distinct objects, one of which is distinguished as the first coordinate and the other as the second coordinate.
   a. Ordered pair0
   b. Thing
   c. Undefined
   d. Undefined

3. In mathematics, the conjugate _____ or adjoint matrix of an m-by-n matrix A with complex entries is the n-by-m matrix A* obtained from A by taking the transpose and then taking the complex conjugate of each entry.
   a. Pairs0
   b. Thing
   c. Undefined
   d. Undefined

4. The mathematical concept of a _____ expresses the intuitive idea of deterministic dependence between two quantities, one of which is viewed as primary and the other as secondary. A _____ then is a way to associate a unique output for each input of a specified type, for example, a real number or an element of a given set.
   a. Function0
   b. Thing
   c. Undefined
   d. Undefined

5. In mathematics, a _____ of a k-place relation $L \subseteq X_1 \times ... \times X_k$ is one of the sets X_j, $1 \leq j \leq k$. In the special case where k = 2 and $L \subseteq X_1 \times X_2$ is a function $L : X_1 \to X_2$, it is conventional to refer to X_1 as the _____ of the function and to refer to X_2 as the codomain of the function.
   a. Thing
   b. Domain0
   c. Undefined
   d. Undefined

6. In mathematics, the _____ of a function is the set of all "output" values produced by that function. Given a function $f : A \to B$, the _____ of f, is defined to be the set $\{x \in B : x = f(a) \text{ for some } a \in A\}$.
   a. Range0
   b. Thing
   c. Undefined
   d. Undefined

7. In mathematics, a _____ of a number x is the exponent y of the power by such that $x = b^y$. The value used for the base b must be neither 0 nor 1, nor a root of 1 in the case of the extension to complex numbers, and is typically 10, e, or 2.
   a. Logarithm0
   b. Thing
   c. Undefined
   d. Undefined

Chapter 7. Calculus of Several Variables

8. Fixed costs are expenses whose total does not change in proportion to the activity of a business. Unit fixed costs decline with volume following a retangular hyperbola as the volume of production. Variable costs by contrast change in relation to the activity of a business such as sales or production volume. Along with variable costs, fixed costs make up one of the two components of total cost. In the most simple production function total cost is equal to fixed costs plus variable costs. In accounting terminology, fixed costs will broadly include all costs which are not included in cost of goods sold, and variable costs are those captured in costs of goods sold. The implicit assumption required to make the equivalence between the accounting and economics terminology is that the accounting period is equal to the period in which fixed costs do not vary in relation to production. In practice, this equivalence does not always hold and depending on the period under consideration by management, some overhead expenses can be adjusted by management, and the specific allocation of each expense to each category will be decided under cost accounting. In business planning and management accounting, usage of the terms fixed costs, variable costs and others will often differ from usage in economics, and may depend on the intended use. For example, costs may be segregated into per unit costs fixed costs per period, and variable costs as a proportion of revenue. Capital expenditures will usually be allocated separately, and depending on the purpose, a portion may be regularly allocated to expenses as depreciation and amortization and seen as a _____ per period, or the entire amount may be considered upfront fixed costs.
    a. Thing
    b. Fixed cost0
    c. Undefined
    d. Undefined

9. _____ are expenses whose total does not change in proportion to the activity of a business, within the relevant time period or scale of production
    a. Thing
    b. Fixed costs0
    c. Undefined
    d. Undefined

10. _____ asserts that the maximum output of a technologically-determined production process is a mathematical function of input factors of production.
    a. Production function0
    b. Thing
    c. Undefined
    d. Undefined

11. The _____ of measurement are a globally standardized and modernized form of the metric system.
    a. Thing
    b. Units0
    c. Undefined
    d. Undefined

12. _____ is a term applied when talking about the movement of air from one place to the next.
    a. Thing
    b. Wind speed0
    c. Undefined
    d. Undefined

13. _____ is a temperature scale named after the German physicist Daniel Gabriel _____ , who proposed it in 1724.
    a. Thing
    b. Fahrenheit0
    c. Undefined
    d. Undefined

14. The word _____ is used in a variety of ways in mathematics.
    a. Thing
    b. Index0
    c. Undefined
    d. Undefined

15. A _____ is a function that assigns a number to subsets of a given set.

Chapter 7. Calculus of Several Variables

    a. Thing
    c. Undefined
    b. Measure0
    d. Undefined

16. In mathematics, there are several meanings of _____ depending on the subject.
    a. Degree0
    c. Undefined
    b. Thing
    d. Undefined

17. _____ is a physical property of a system that underlies the common notions of hot and cold; something that is hotter has the greater _____.
    a. Temperature0
    c. Undefined
    b. Thing
    d. Undefined

18. A _____ is a unit of length, usually used to measure distance, in a number of different systems, including Imperial units, United States customary units and Norwegian/Swedish mil. Its size can vary from system to system, but in each is between 1 and 10 kilometers. In contemporary English contexts _____ refers to either:
    a. Thing
    c. Undefined
    b. Mile0
    d. Undefined

19. _____ is a unit of speed, expressing the number of international miles covered per hour.
    a. Miles per hour0
    c. Undefined
    b. Thing
    d. Undefined

20. In plane geometry, a _____ is a polygon with four equal sides, four right angles, and parallel opposite sides. In algebra, the _____ of a number is that number multiplied by itself.
    a. Thing
    c. Undefined
    b. Square0
    d. Undefined

21. In mathematics, a _____ of a number x is a number r such that $r^2 = x$, or in words, a number r whose square (the result of multiplying the number by itself) is x.
    a. Square root0
    c. Undefined
    b. Thing
    d. Undefined

22. In mathematics, a _____ of a complex-valued function f is a member x of the domain of f such that f(x) vanishes at x, that is, x : f (x) = 0.
    a. Thing
    c. Undefined
    b. Root0
    d. Undefined

23. A _____ is the part of a fraction that tells how many equal parts make up a whole, and which is used in the name of the fraction: "halves", "thirds", "fourths" or "quarters", "fifths" and so on.
    a. Denominator0
    c. Undefined
    b. Concept
    d. Undefined

24. The _____ of a solid object is the three-dimensional concept of how much space it occupies, often quantified numerically.

Chapter 7. Calculus of Several Variables

a. Volume0
c. Undefined
b. Thing
d. Undefined

25. An _____ is a straight line around which a geometric figure can be rotated.
a. Thing
b. Axis0
c. Undefined
d. Undefined

26. A _____ is a set of numbers that designate location in a given reference system, such as x,y in a planar _____ system or an x,y,z in a three-dimensional _____ system.
a. Coordinate0
b. Thing
c. Undefined
d. Undefined

27. In mathematics and its applications, a _____ is a system for assigning an n-tuple of numbers or scalars to each point in an n-dimensional space.
a. Concept
b. Coordinate system0
c. Undefined
d. Undefined

28. In mathematics, the _____ of a coordinate system is the point where the axes of the system intersect.
a. Thing
b. Origin0
c. Undefined
d. Undefined

29. _____ are the basic objects of study in graph theory. Informally speaking, a graph is a set of objects called points, nodes, or vertices connected by links called lines or edges.
a. Graphs0
b. Thing
c. Undefined
d. Undefined

30. In mathematics, the _____ f is the collection of all ordered pairs . In particular, graph means the graphical representation of this collection, in the form of a curve or surface, together with axes, etc. Graphing on a Cartesian plane is sometimes referred to as curve sketching.
a. Thing
b. Graph of a function0
c. Undefined
d. Undefined

31. An _____ or an extremal point is a point that belongs to the extremity of something.
a. Thing
b. Extreme point0
c. Undefined
d. Undefined

32. In the most general terms, a _____ for a smooth function (curve, surface or hypersurface) is a point such that the curve/surface/etc. in the neighborhood of this point lies on different sides of the tangent at this point. In certain contexts the definition may vary. It is most frequently used at critical points.
a. Thing
b. Saddle point0
c. Undefined
d. Undefined

33. The _____ is the highest point in a certain portion of a graph.
a. Thing
b. Relative maximum0
c. Undefined
d. Undefined

Chapter 7. Calculus of Several Variables

34. The _____ is the lowest point in a certain portion of a graph.
    a. Relative minimum0
    b. Thing
    c. Undefined
    d. Undefined

35. A _____ is a landform that extends above the surrounding terrain in a limited area. A _____ is generally steeper than a hill, but there is no universally accepted standard definition for the height of a _____ or a hill although a _____ usually has an identifiable summit.
    a. Thing
    b. Mountain0
    c. Undefined
    d. Undefined

36. An _____ is a combination of numbers, operators, grouping symbols and/or free variables and bound variables arranged in a meaningful way which can be evaluated..
    a. Thing
    b. Expression0
    c. Undefined
    d. Undefined

37. _____ is a payment made by a company to its shareholders
    a. Dividend0
    b. Thing
    c. Undefined
    d. Undefined

38. _____, in economics and political economy, are the distributions or payments awarded to the various suppliers of the factors of production.
    a. Thing
    b. Returns0
    c. Undefined
    d. Undefined

39. _____ is a kind of property which exists as magnitude or multitude. It is among the basic classes of things along with quality, substance, change, and relation.
    a. Thing
    b. Amount0
    c. Undefined
    d. Undefined

40. In Euclidean geometry, a uniform _____ is a linear transformation that enlargers or diminishes objects, and whose _____ factor is the same in all directions. This is also called homothethy.
    a. Thing
    b. Scale0
    c. Undefined
    d. Undefined

41. In sociology and biology a _____ is the collection of people or organisms of a particular species living in a given geographic area or space, usually measured by a census.
    a. Thing
    b. Population0
    c. Undefined
    d. Undefined

42. The _____ or kilogramme is the SI base unit of mass. It is defined as being equal to the mass of the international prototype of the _____.
    a. Thing
    b. Kilogram0
    c. Undefined
    d. Undefined

43. _____ is, or relates to, the _____ temperature scale .

Chapter 7. Calculus of Several Variables

a. Thing
b. Celsius0
c. Undefined
d. Undefined

44. _____ of a function of several variables is its derivative with respect to one of those variables with the others held constant as opposed to the total derivative, in which all variables are allowed to vary.
a. Thing
b. Partial derivative0
c. Undefined
d. Undefined

45. The _____ is a measurement of how a function changes when the values of its inputs change.
a. Thing
b. Derivative0
c. Undefined
d. Undefined

46. In mathematics and the mathematical sciences, a _____ is a fixed, but possibly unspecified, value. This is in contrast to a variable, which is not fixed.
a. Constant0
b. Thing
c. Undefined
d. Undefined

47. _____ has many meanings, most of which simply .
a. Thing
b. Power0
c. Undefined
d. Undefined

48. In mathematics, a _____ is the end result of a division problem. It can also be expressed as the number of times the divisor divides into the dividend.
a. Quotient0
b. Thing
c. Undefined
d. Undefined

49. _____ is a method for differentiating expressions involving exponentiation the power operation.
a. Power rule0
b. Thing
c. Undefined
d. Undefined

50. In mathematics, _____ expressions is used to reduce the expression into the lowest possible term.
a. Simplifying0
b. Thing
c. Undefined
d. Undefined

51. The _____ is a method of finding the derivative of a function that is the quotient of two other functions for which derivatives exist.
a. Thing
b. Quotient rule0
c. Undefined
d. Undefined

52. The _____, the average in everyday English, which is also called the arithmetic _____ (and is distinguished from the geometric _____ or harmonic _____). The average is also called the sample _____. The expected value of a random variable, which is also called the population _____.
a. Thing
b. Mean0
c. Undefined
d. Undefined

Chapter 7. Calculus of Several Variables

53. _____, a field in mathematics, is the study of how functions change when their inputs change. The primary object of study in _____ is the derivative.
   a. Thing
   b. Differential calculus0
   c. Undefined
   d. Undefined

54. A _____ is a special kind of ratio, indicating a relationship between two measurements with different units, such as miles to gallons or cents to pounds.
   a. Thing
   b. Rate0
   c. Undefined
   d. Undefined

55. In mathematics, a _____ is the result of multiplying, or an expression that identifies factors to be multiplied.
   a. Product0
   b. Thing
   c. Undefined
   d. Undefined

56. _____, from Latin meaning "to make progress", is defined in two different ways. Pure economic _____ is the increase in wealth that an investor has from making an investment, taking into consideration all costs associated with that investment including the opportunity cost of capital.
   a. Profit0
   b. Thing
   c. Undefined
   d. Undefined

57. In common philosophical language, a proposition or _____, is the content of an assertion, that is, it is true-or-false and defined by the meaning of a particular piece of language.
   a. Concept
   b. Statement0
   c. Undefined
   d. Undefined

58. _____ is the change in total cost that arises when the quantity produced changes by one unit.
   a. Thing
   b. Marginal cost0
   c. Undefined
   d. Undefined

59. _____ is a business term for the amount of money that a company receives from its activities in a given period, mostly from sales of products and/or services to customers
   a. Revenue0
   b. Thing
   c. Undefined
   d. Undefined

60. Mathematical _____ is used to represent ideas.
   a. Notation0
   b. Thing
   c. Undefined
   d. Undefined

61. A _____ function is a function for which, intuitively, small changes in the input result in small changes in the output.
   a. Continuous0
   b. Event
   c. Undefined
   d. Undefined

62. _____ is a mathematical subject that includes the study of limits, derivatives, integrals, and power series and constitutes a major part of modern university curriculum.

Chapter 7. Calculus of Several Variables

    a. Calculus0
    c. Undefined
    b. Thing
    d. Undefined

63. _____ is a form of periodic payment from an employer to an employee, which is specified in an employment contract.
    a. Thing
    c. Undefined
    b. Gross pay0
    d. Undefined

64. In mathematics, an _____, mean, or central tendency of a data set refers to a measure of the "middle" or "expected" value of the data set.
    a. Concept
    c. Undefined
    b. Average0
    d. Undefined

65. A _____ is a form of periodic payment from an employer to an employee, which is specified in an employment contract.
    a. Thing
    c. Undefined
    b. Salary0
    d. Undefined

66. In classical geometry, a _____ of a circle or sphere is any line segment from its center to its boundary. By extension, the _____ of a circle or sphere is the length of any such segment. The _____ is half the diameter. In science and engineering the term _____ of curvature is commonly used as a synonym for _____.
    a. Thing
    c. Undefined
    b. Radius0
    d. Undefined

67. _____ is the flow of blood in the cardiovascular system.
    a. Thing
    c. Undefined
    b. Blood flow0
    d. Undefined

68. _____ of an object is its speed in a particular direction.
    a. Velocity0
    c. Undefined
    b. Thing
    d. Undefined

69. A pair of angles are _____ if the sum of their angles is 90°.
    a. Concept
    c. Undefined
    b. Complementary0
    d. Undefined

70. _____ is often used to describe the measurement of the steepness, incline, gradient, or grade of a straight line. The _____ is defined as the ratio of the "rise" divided by the "run" between two points on a line, or in other words, the ratio of the altitude change to the horizontal distance between any two points on the line.
    a. Slope0
    c. Undefined
    b. Thing
    d. Undefined

71. _____ is a point on the domain of a function
    a. Critical point0
    c. Undefined
    b. Thing
    d. Undefined

Chapter 7. Calculus of Several Variables

72. Acid _____ ratio measures the ability of a company to use its near cash or quick assets to immediately extinguish its current liabilities.
    a. Thing
    b. Test0
    c. Undefined
    d. Undefined

73. The term _____ refers to the largest and the smallest element of a set.
    a. Extreme value0
    b. Thing
    c. Undefined
    d. Undefined

74. In mathematics, a _____ is an expression that is constructed from one or more variables and constants, using only the operations of addition, subtraction, multiplication, and constant positive whole number exponents. is a _____. Note in particular that division by an expression containing a variable is not in general allowed in polynomials. [1]
    a. Thing
    b. Polynomial0
    c. Undefined
    d. Undefined

75. In mathematics, a subset of Euclidean space R^n is called _____ if it is closed and bounded.
    a. Thing
    b. Compact0
    c. Undefined
    d. Undefined

76. U.S. liquid _____ is legally defined as 231 cubic inches, and is equal to 3.785411784 litres or abotu 0.13368 cubic feet. This is the most common definition of a _____. The U.S. fluid ounce is defined as 1/128 of a U.S. _____.
    a. Gallon0
    b. Thing
    c. Undefined
    d. Undefined

77. A _____ is an individual or household that purchases and uses goods and services generated within the economy.
    a. Consumer0
    b. Thing
    c. Undefined
    d. Undefined

78. The plus and _____ signs are mathematical symbols used to represent the notions of positive and negative as well as the operations of addition and subtraction.
    a. Thing
    b. Minus0
    c. Undefined
    d. Undefined

79. In mathematics, the concept of a _____ tries to capture the intuitive idea of a geometrical one-dimensional and continuous object. A simple example is the circle.
    a. Thing
    b. Curve0
    c. Undefined
    d. Undefined

80. _____ is a synonym for information.
    a. Data0
    b. Thing
    c. Undefined
    d. Undefined

81. In mathematics, _____ are the intuitive idea of a geometrical one-dimensional and continuous object.

Chapter 7. Calculus of Several Variables

    a. Curves0
    b. Thing
    c. Undefined
    d. Undefined

82. In regression analysis, _____, also known as ordinary _____ analysis is a method for linear regression that determines the values of unknown quantities in a statistical model by minimizing the sum of the residuals difference between the predicted and observed values squared.
    a. Least squares0
    b. Thing
    c. Undefined
    d. Undefined

83. In business, particularly accounting, a _____ is the time intervals that the accounts, statement, payments, or other calculations cover.
    a. Thing
    b. Period0
    c. Undefined
    d. Undefined

84. A _____ is the result of the addition of a set of numbers. The numbers may be natural numbers, complex numbers, matrices, or still more complicated objects. An infinite _____ is a subtle procedure known as a series.
    a. Thing
    b. Sum0
    c. Undefined
    d. Undefined

85. _____ is a measure of difference for interval and ratio variables between the observed value and the mean.
    a. Deviation0
    b. Thing
    c. Undefined
    d. Undefined

86. In statistics, _____ are observations that are numerically distant from the rest of the data.
    a. Thing
    b. Outliers0
    c. Undefined
    d. Undefined

87. In mathematics, _____ growth occurs when the growth rate of a function is always proportional to the function's current size.
    a. Exponential0
    b. Thing
    c. Undefined
    d. Undefined

88. _____ is the logarithm to the base e, where e is an irrational constant approximately equal to 2.718281828459.
    a. Thing
    b. Natural logarithm0
    c. Undefined
    d. Undefined

89. In geometry, the _____ of an object is a point in some sense in the middle of the object.
    a. Thing
    b. Center0
    c. Undefined
    d. Undefined

90. _____ is a statistical measure of the average length of survival of a living thing.
    a. Thing
    b. Life expectancy0
    c. Undefined
    d. Undefined

91. _____ is the chance that something is likely to happen or be the case.

a. Probability0
b. Thing
c. Undefined
d. Undefined

92. The word _____ comes from the Latin word linearis, which means created by lines.
a. Linear0
b. Thing
c. Undefined
d. Undefined

93. _____ is a regression method that models the relationship between a dependent variable Y, independent variables Xp, and a random term à.
a. Linear regression0
b. Thing
c. Undefined
d. Undefined

94. _____ are a method for finding the extrema of a function of several variables subject to one or more constraints: it is the basic tool in nonlinear constrained optimization.
a. Thing
b. Lagrange multipliers0
c. Undefined
d. Undefined

95. In mathematics, a _____ is a condition that a solution to an optimization problem must satisfy in order to be acceptable.
a. Constraint0
b. Thing
c. Undefined
d. Undefined

96. In geometry, a _____ (Greek words diairo = divide and metro = measure) of a circle is any straight line segment that passes through the centre and whose endpoints are on the circular boundary, or, in more modern usage, the length of such a line segment. When using the word in the more modern sense, one speaks of the _____ rather than a _____, because all diameters of a circle have the same length. This length is twice the radius. The _____ of a circle is also the longest chord that the circle has.
a. Thing
b. Diameter0
c. Undefined
d. Undefined

97. _____ traditionally refers to the statistical process of determining comparable scores on different forms of an exam
a. Equating0
b. Thing
c. Undefined
d. Undefined

98. In combinatorial mathematics, a _____ is an un-ordered collection of unique elements.
a. Combination0
b. Concept
c. Undefined
d. Undefined

99. In mathematics, _____ is the decomposition of an object into a product of other objects, or factors, which when multiplied together give the original.
a. Thing
b. Factoring0
c. Undefined
d. Undefined

100. Equivalence is the condition of being _____ or essentially equal.

Chapter 7. Calculus of Several Variables

a. Thing
b. Equivalent0
c. Undefined
d. Undefined

101. _____ is a branch of mathematics concerning the study of structure, relation and quantity.
a. Concept
b. Algebra0
c. Undefined
d. Undefined

102. In mathematics, the _____ (or modulus) of a real number is its numerical value without regard to its sign.
a. Absolute value0
b. Thing
c. Undefined
d. Undefined

103. _____ is a set, with some particular properties and usually some additional structure, such as the operations of addition or multiplication, for instance.
a. Thing
b. Space0
c. Undefined
d. Undefined

104. A _____ is traditionally an infinitesimally small change in a variable.
a. Thing
b. Differential0
c. Undefined
d. Undefined

105. In mathematics, an _____ is any of the arguments, i.e. "inputs", to a function. Thus if we have a function f(x), then x is a _____.
a. Independent variable0
b. Thing
c. Undefined
d. Undefined

106. _____ is an approximation of a general function using a linear function more precisely, an affine function.
a. Linear approximation0
b. Thing
c. Undefined
d. Undefined

107. _____ are objects, characters, or other concrete representations of ideas, concepts, or other abstractions.
a. Thing
b. Symbols0
c. Undefined
d. Undefined

108. _____ comes from the Latin word linearis, which means created by lines.
a. Thing
b. Linearity0
c. Undefined
d. Undefined

109. _____ is an interpreted dynamic visual programming language based on Squeak, a smalltalk implementation directly derived from Smalltalk-80.
a. Scratch0
b. Thing
c. Undefined
d. Undefined

110. The act of _____ is the calculated approximation of a result which is usable even if input data may be incomplete, uncertain, or noisy.

Chapter 7. Calculus of Several Variables

a. Thing
c. Undefined
b. Estimating0
d. Undefined

111. _____ is the application of tools and a processing medium to the transformation of raw materials into finished goods for sale.
   a. Thing
   c. Undefined
   b. Manufacturing0
   d. Undefined

112. _____ is the estimation of a physical quantity such as distance, energy, temperature, or time.
   a. Measurement0
   c. Undefined
   b. Thing
   d. Undefined

113. A _____ is a deliberate process for transforming one or more inputs into one or more results.
   a. Calculation0
   c. Undefined
   b. Thing
   d. Undefined

114. In mathematics, a _____ is a quadric surface, with the following equation in Cartesian coordinates: $(x/_a)^2 + (y/_b)^2 = 1$.
   a. Thing
   c. Undefined
   b. Cylinder0
   d. Undefined

115. _____ is a way of expressing a number as a fraction of 100 per cent meaning "per hundred".
   a. Thing
   c. Undefined
   b. Percent0
   d. Undefined

116. A _____ is a quantity that denotes the proportional amount or magnitude of one quantity relative to another.
   a. Thing
   c. Undefined
   b. Ratio0
   d. Undefined

117. In botany, _____ are above-ground plant organs specialized for photosynthesis. Their characteristics are typically analyzed by using Fiobonacci's sequences.
   a. Leaves0
   c. Undefined
   b. Thing
   d. Undefined

118. In geometry, a _____ is defined as a quadrilateral where all four of its angles are right angles.
   a. Thing
   c. Undefined
   b. Rectangle0
   d. Undefined

119. _____ are a measure of time.
   a. Minutes0
   c. Undefined
   b. Thing
   d. Undefined

120. In the mathematical field of numerical analysis, the _____ in some data is the discrepancy between an exact value and some approximation to it.

Chapter 7. Calculus of Several Variables

a. Approximation Error0
b. Thing
c. Undefined
d. Undefined

121. In mathematics, _____ geometry was the traditional name for the geometry of three-dimensional Euclidean space — for practical purposes the kind of space we live in.
a. Solid0
b. Thing
c. Undefined
d. Undefined

122. _____ is the volume of blood being pumped by the heart, in particular a ventricle in a minute.
a. Cardiac output0
b. Thing
c. Undefined
d. Undefined

123. The existence and properties of _____ are the basis of Euclid's parallel postulate. _____ are two lines on the same plane that do not intersect even assuming that lines extend to infinity in either direction.
a. Thing
b. Parallel lines0
c. Undefined
d. Undefined

124. A _____ of a number is the product of that number with any integer.
a. Thing
b. Multiple0
c. Undefined
d. Undefined

125. The _____ of a function is an extension of the concept of a sum, and are identified or found through the use of integration.
a. Thing
b. Integral0
c. Undefined
d. Undefined

126. The _____ integers are all the integers from zero on upwards.
a. Thing
b. Nonnegative0
c. Undefined
d. Undefined

127. _____ is a process of combining or accumulating. It may also refer to:
a. Thing
b. Integration0
c. Undefined
d. Undefined

128. In mathematical analysis and related areas of mathematics, a set is called _____, if it is, in a certain sense, of finite size.
a. Thing
b. Bounded0
c. Undefined
d. Undefined

129. In mathematics, a _____ is an n-tuple with n being 3.
a. Triple0
b. Thing
c. Undefined
d. Undefined

130. _____ is mass m per unit volume V.

Chapter 7. Calculus of Several Variables

a. Density0
b. Thing
c. Undefined
d. Undefined

131. A _____ is a statement or claimt that a particular event will occur in the future in more certain terms than a forecast.
   a. Thing
   b. Prediction0
   c. Undefined
   d. Undefined

132. In computer science, an _____ is the problem of finding the best solution from all feasible solutions.
   a. Optimization problem0
   b. Thing
   c. Undefined
   d. Undefined

133. _____ represents the combinations of goods and services that a consumer can purchase given current prices and his income.
   a. Thing
   b. Budget constraint0
   c. Undefined
   d. Undefined

134. In geometry, an _____ of a triangle is a straight line through a vertex and perpendicular to (i.e. forming a right angle with) the opposite side or an extension of the opposite side.
   a. Concept
   b. Altitude0
   c. Undefined
   d. Undefined

135. _____ is a a point on a curve at which the tangent crosses the curve itself.
   a. Thing
   b. Inflection point0
   c. Undefined
   d. Undefined

136. A _____ is a simplified and structured visual representation of concepts, ideas, constructions, relations, statistical data, anatomy etc used in all aspects of human activities to visualize and clarify the topic.
   a. Thing
   b. Diagram0
   c. Undefined
   d. Undefined

137. An _____ is a straight line or curve A to which another curve B approaches closer and closer as one moves along it. As one moves along B, the space between it and the _____ A becomes smaller and smaller, and can in fact be made as small as one could wish by going far enough along. A curve may or may not touch or cross its _____. In fact, the curve may intersect the _____ an infinite number of times.
   a. Asymptote0
   b. Thing
   c. Undefined
   d. Undefined

138. _____ is the fee paid on borrowed money.
   a. Interest0
   b. Thing
   c. Undefined
   d. Undefined

139. In elementary algebra, an _____ is a set that contains every real number between two indicated numbers and may contain the two numbers themselves.

Chapter 7. Calculus of Several Variables

a. Interval0
b. Thing
c. Undefined
d. Undefined

140. A _____ is a negotiable instrument instructing a financial institution to pay a specific amount of a specific currency from a specific demand account held in the maker/depositor's name with that institution. Both the maker and payee may be natural persons or legal entities.
   a. Thing
   b. Check0
   c. Undefined
   d. Undefined

141. A _____ is a quadrilateral, which is defined as a shape with four sides, which has a pair of parallel sides.
   a. Trapezoid0
   b. Thing
   c. Undefined
   d. Undefined

142. Regrouping is the act of putting ones into groups of 10. For example, the 1 on the far right of 131 would be denoted _____ if the digit of the number being subtracted is larger than 1, such as 131-99.
   a. By 100
   b. Thing
   c. Undefined
   d. Undefined

143. Any point where a graph makes contact with an coordinate axis is called an _____ of the graph
   a. Intercept0
   b. Thing
   c. Undefined
   d. Undefined

144. In geometry, a line _____ is a part of a line that is bounded by two end points, and contains every point on the line between its end points.
   a. Segment0
   b. Concept
   c. Undefined
   d. Undefined

145. In geometry, an _____ is a point at which a line segment or ray terminates.
   a. Thing
   b. Endpoint0
   c. Undefined
   d. Undefined

146. A _____ is a part of a line that is bounded by two end points, and contains every point on the line between its end points.
   a. Thing
   b. Line segment0
   c. Undefined
   d. Undefined

147. The _____ are the only integral domain whose positive elements are well-ordered, and in which order is preserved by addition. Like the natural numbers, the _____ form a countably infinite set. The set of all _____ is usually denoted in mathematics by a boldface Z .
   a. Integers0
   b. Thing
   c. Undefined
   d. Undefined

148. In geometry, a _____ is a special kind of point, usually a corner of a polygon, polyhedron, or higher dimensional polytope. In the geometry of curves a _____ is a point of where the first derivative of curvature is zero. In graph theory, a _____ is the fundamental unit out of which graphs are formed

Chapter 7. Calculus of Several Variables

a. Vertex0
b. Thing
c. Undefined
d. Undefined

149. In mathematics, the _____ is a conic section generated by the intersection of a right circular conical surface and a plane parallel to a generating straight line of that surface. It can also be defined as locus of points in a plane which are equidistant from a given point.
   a. Thing
   b. Parabola0
   c. Undefined
   d. Undefined

150. In astronomy, geography, geometry and related sciences and contexts, a plane is said to be _____ at a given point if it is locally perpendicular to the gradient of the gravity field, i.e., with the direction of the gravitational force at that point.
   a. Thing
   b. Horizontal0
   c. Undefined
   d. Undefined

151. _____ is a function whose values do not vary and thus are constant.
   a. Constant function0
   b. Thing
   c. Undefined
   d. Undefined

152. In mathematics, defined and _____ are used to explain whether or not expressions have meaningful, sensible, and unambiguous values.
   a. Thing
   b. Undefined0
   c. Undefined
   d. Undefined

153. In mathematics, a _____ is a two-dimensional manifold or surface that is perfectly flat.
   a. Thing
   b. Plane0
   c. Undefined
   d. Undefined

154. In mathematics, _____ are two-dimensional manifolds or surfaces that are perfectly flat.
   a. Planes0
   b. Thing
   c. Undefined
   d. Undefined

155. Compass and straightedge or ruler-and-compass _____ is the _____ of lengths or angles using only an idealized ruler and compass.
   a. Thing
   b. Construction0
   c. Undefined
   d. Undefined

156. The _____ is the distance around a closed curve. _____ is a kind of perimeter.
   a. Circumference0
   b. Thing
   c. Undefined
   d. Undefined

157. _____ is defined as the rate of change or derivative with respect to time of velocity.
   a. Thing
   b. Acceleration0
   c. Undefined
   d. Undefined

Chapter 7. Calculus of Several Variables

158. In trigonometry, the _____ is a function defined as $\tan x = \sin x / \cos x$. The function is so-named because it can be defined as the length of a certain segment of a _____ (in the geometric sense) to the unit circle. In plane geometry, a line is _____ to a curve, at some point, if both line and curve pass through the point with the same direction.
   a. Tangent0
   b. Thing
   c. Undefined
   d. Undefined

159. _____ has two distinct but etymologically-related meanings: one in geometry and one in trigonometry.
   a. Thing
   b. Tangent line0
   c. Undefined
   d. Undefined

160. In mathematics, _____ refers to the rewriting of an expression into a simpler form.
   a. Reduction0
   b. Thing
   c. Undefined
   d. Undefined

161. _____ is the distance around a given two-dimensional object. As a general rule, the _____ of a polygon can always be calculated by adding all the length of the sides together. So, the formula for triangles is $P = a + b + c$, where a, b and c stand for each side of it. For quadrilaterals the equation is $P = a + b + c + d$. For equilateral polygons, $P = na$, where n is the number of sides and a is the side length.
   a. Thing
   b. Perimeter0
   c. Undefined
   d. Undefined

162. In geometry, two lines or planes if one falls on the other in such a way as to create congruent adjacent angles. The term may be used as a noun or adjective. Thus, referring to Figure 1, the line AB is the _____ to CD through the point B.
   a. Perpendicular0
   b. Thing
   c. Undefined
   d. Undefined

163. In mathematics, _____ are used in a variety of notations, including standard notations for intervals, commutators, the Lie bracket, and the Iverson bracket.
   a. Thing
   b. Square Brackets0
   c. Undefined
   d. Undefined

164. _____ is the transport of people on a trip/journey or the process or time involved in a person or object moving from one location to another.
   a. Thing
   b. Travel0
   c. Undefined
   d. Undefined

165. _____ is the name for any one of many units of measure used by various ancient peoples and is among the first recorded units of length.
   a. Cubit0
   b. Thing
   c. Undefined
   d. Undefined

166. _____ generally derives from name. A _____ quantity e.g., length, diameter, volume, voltage, value is generally the quantity according to which some item has been named or is generally referred to.
   a. Nominal0
   b. Thing
   c. Undefined
   d. Undefined

Chapter 7. Calculus of Several Variables

167. The _____ (symbol _____) and the millibar (symbol mbar, also mb) are units of pressure.
   a. Bar0
   b. Thing
   c. Undefined
   d. Undefined

168. _____ is the process of reducing the number of significant digits in a number.
   a. Concept
   b. Rounding0
   c. Undefined
   d. Undefined

169. _____ is the middle point of a line segment.
   a. Thing
   b. Midpoint0
   c. Undefined
   d. Undefined

170. _____ is a function that extends the concept of an ordinary sum
   a. Thing
   b. Integrand0
   c. Undefined
   d. Undefined

171. The metre (or _____, see spelling differences) is a measure of length. It is the basic unit of length in the metric system and in the International System of Units (SI), used around the world for general and scientific purposes.
   a. Meter0
   b. Concept
   c. Undefined
   d. Undefined

172. In mathematics, a _____ series is an infinite series that is not convergent, meaning that the infinite sequence of the partial sums of the series does not have a limit.
   a. Divergent0
   b. Thing
   c. Undefined
   d. Undefined

ANSWER KEY

Chapter 1

1. b	2. b	3. b	4. a	5. a	6. a	7. b	8. a	9. a	10. b
11. b	12. b	13. a	14. b	15. a	16. b	17. b	18. a	19. b	20. b
21. a	22. a	23. b	24. b	25. a	26. a	27. a	28. a	29. b	30. a
31. a	32. a	33. b	34. a	35. a	36. a	37. a	38. b	39. b	40. a
41. b	42. b	43. a	44. a	45. b	46. a	47. b	48. a	49. a	50. b
51. b	52. a	53. b	54. b	55. b	56. b	57. a	58. b	59. b	60. b
61. b	62. a	63. a	64. a	65. b	66. a	67. a	68. b	69. b	70. a
71. a	72. a	73. b	74. a	75. b	76. b	77. b	78. a	79. b	80. b
81. b	82. b	83. a	84. b	85. a	86. a	87. b	88. a	89. a	90. b
91. b	92. a	93. b	94. a	95. a	96. a	97. a	98. a	99. b	100. b
101. a	102. a	103. a	104. a	105. a	106. b	107. b	108. b	109. a	110. b
111. a	112. b	113. b	114. a	115. b	116. b	117. b	118. b	119. a	120. b
121. a	122. b	123. a	124. a	125. b	126. a	127. a	128. b	129. b	130. a
131. a	132. a	133. b	134. b	135. a	136. b	137. b	138. b	139. b	140. a
141. b	142. b	143. b	144. a	145. b	146. b	147. b	148. b	149. b	150. b
151. a	152. b	153. a	154. b	155. b	156. b	157. a	158. b	159. a	160. b
161. a	162. a	163. b							

Chapter 2

1. a	2. a	3. a	4. b	5. a	6. a	7. a	8. b	9. a	10. b
11. a	12. b	13. a	14. b	15. b	16. b	17. b	18. a	19. a	20. a
21. b	22. a	23. a	24. a	25. a	26. a	27. b	28. a	29. b	30. b
31. b	32. a	33. b	34. a	35. a	36. b	37. a	38. a	39. b	40. a
41. a	42. b	43. a	44. b	45. a	46. a	47. a	48. b	49. a	50. a
51. a	52. a	53. b	54. b	55. a	56. a	57. b	58. a	59. a	60. a
61. b	62. b	63. b	64. a	65. a	66. a	67. b	68. b	69. b	70. a
71. b	72. a	73. a	74. b	75. a	76. a	77. b	78. b	79. b	80. a
81. a	82. a	83. a	84. a	85. b	86. a	87. a	88. a	89. b	90. b
91. b	92. b	93. b	94. a	95. b	96. b	97. a	98. a	99. b	100. b
101. a	102. b	103. a	104. a	105. a	106. b	107. b	108. b	109. a	110. b
111. b	112. b	113. a	114. a	115. b	116. b	117. b	118. b	119. a	120. b
121. a	122. a	123. a	124. a	125. a	126. b	127. b	128. b	129. a	130. a
131. b	132. b	133. a	134. a	135. a	136. a	137. b	138. b	139. a	140. b
141. b	142. a								

Chapter 3

1. a	2. b	3. a	4. b	5. a	6. a	7. b	8. b	9. a	10. b
11. b	12. a	13. b	14. b	15. a	16. a	17. b	18. b	19. b	20. b
21. a	22. a	23. b	24. b	25. a	26. a	27. b	28. a	29. b	30. a
31. b	32. b	33. b	34. a	35. a	36. a	37. b	38. b	39. a	40. a
41. a	42. b	43. b	44. a	45. b	46. b	47. a	48. a	49. b	50. b
51. b	52. a	53. a	54. b	55. a	56. b	57. b	58. a	59. a	60. a
61. b	62. b	63. b	64. b	65. b	66. a	67. b	68. b	69. a	70. b
71. a	72. b	73. b	74. a	75. b	76. a	77. b	78. a	79. a	80. b
81. b	82. a	83. b	84. b	85. a	86. b	87. a	88. b	89. b	90. a
91. a	92. a	93. b	94. a	95. b	96. b	97. a	98. b	99. b	100. a
101. a	102. a	103. b	104. a	105. b	106. b	107. a	108. a	109. b	110. b
111. a	112. a	113. a	114. a	115. a	116. b	117. a	118. b	119. b	120. a
121. b	122. a	123. a	124. b	125. a	126. a	127. a	128. b	129. b	130. a
131. b	132. a	133. b	134. a	135. a	136. a				

Chapter 4

1. a	2. a	3. b	4. a	5. a	6. a	7. b	8. a	9. a	10. a
11. b	12. b	13. a	14. a	15. a	16. b	17. b	18. b	19. a	20. a
21. a	22. a	23. b	24. b	25. b	26. b	27. a	28. a	29. a	30. b
31. a	32. a	33. a	34. b	35. b	36. b	37. a	38. b	39. a	40. a
41. a	42. a	43. a	44. b	45. a	46. b	47. a	48. a	49. b	50. b
51. a	52. b	53. b	54. b	55. a	56. a	57. a	58. b	59. b	60. b
61. b	62. a	63. b	64. a	65. b	66. a	67. a	68. b	69. b	70. a
71. a	72. b	73. b	74. b	75. b	76. a	77. a	78. b	79. a	80. a
81. a	82. b	83. b	84. a	85. b	86. a	87. b	88. b	89. b	90. b
91. a	92. a	93. a	94. a	95. a	96. a	97. a	98. b	99. a	100. b
101. a	102. a	103. b	104. b	105. a	106. a	107. b	108. b	109. a	110. b
111. a	112. a	113. b	114. b	115. b	116. b	117. a	118. b	119. a	120. a
121. b	122. a	123. a	124. b	125. a	126. b	127. a	128. b	129. b	130. b
131. b	132. a								

ANSWER KEY

Chapter 5

1. b	2. a	3. a	4. b	5. b	6. a	7. b	8. b	9. a	10. b
11. a	12. a	13. b	14. a	15. b	16. a	17. a	18. b	19. a	20. a
21. b	22. a	23. a	24. a	25. a	26. a	27. a	28. b	29. b	30. a
31. b	32. a	33. a	34. b	35. a	36. a	37. b	38. a	39. b	40. a
41. a	42. a	43. a	44. b	45. b	46. b	47. b	48. b	49. b	50. b
51. a	52. a	53. a	54. a	55. a	56. a	57. a	58. b	59. a	60. b
61. a	62. a	63. b	64. b	65. b	66. a	67. b	68. a	69. a	70. a
71. a	72. a	73. a	74. b	75. a	76. b	77. b	78. a	79. a	80. a
81. a	82. a	83. a	84. b	85. a	86. b	87. b	88. b	89. b	90. b
91. b	92. a	93. a	94. b	95. a	96. b	97. b	98. a	99. b	100. b
101. b	102. b	103. a	104. b	105. b	106. a	107. a	108. a	109. b	110. b
111. a	112. b	113. b	114. a	115. b	116. b	117. b	118. b	119. b	120. a
121. a	122. a	123. b	124. a	125. a	126. a	127. b	128. a	129. b	

Chapter 6

1. a	2. b	3. b	4. a	5. b	6. a	7. b	8. b	9. a	10. a
11. b	12. b	13. a	14. b	15. b	16. a	17. a	18. b	19. a	20. a
21. a	22. b	23. a	24. b	25. b	26. b	27. b	28. a	29. a	30. a
31. a	32. b	33. b	34. b	35. b	36. a	37. b	38. a	39. b	40. b
41. b	42. b	43. b	44. b	45. a	46. a	47. a	48. b	49. a	50. b
51. a	52. a	53. b	54. b	55. a	56. a	57. a	58. a	59. b	60. a
61. a	62. b	63. b	64. a	65. b	66. a	67. a	68. b	69. a	70. a
71. a	72. a	73. b	74. b	75. b	76. b	77. a	78. a	79. b	80. b
81. b	82. a	83. b	84. b	85. b	86. a	87. b	88. a	89. b	90. b
91. a	92. b	93. a	94. a	95. b	96. b	97. b	98. b	99. b	100. a
101. a	102. b	103. b	104. a	105. a	106. b	107. b	108. b	109. a	110. b
111. b	112. a	113. a	114. b	115. a	116. a	117. b	118. b	119. a	120. a
121. b	122. b	123. a	124. a	125. b	126. a	127. b	128. a	129. a	130. a
131. a	132. a	133. b	134. a	135. b	136. a	137. a	138. a		

Chapter 7

1. b	2. a	3. a	4. a	5. b	6. a	7. a	8. b	9. b	10. a
11. b	12. b	13. b	14. b	15. b	16. a	17. a	18. b	19. a	20. b
21. a	22. b	23. a	24. a	25. b	26. a	27. b	28. b	29. a	30. b
31. b	32. b	33. b	34. a	35. b	36. b	37. a	38. b	39. b	40. b
41. b	42. b	43. b	44. b	45. b	46. a	47. b	48. a	49. a	50. a
51. b	52. b	53. b	54. b	55. a	56. a	57. b	58. b	59. a	60. a
61. a	62. a	63. b	64. b	65. b	66. b	67. b	68. a	69. b	70. a
71. a	72. b	73. a	74. b	75. b	76. a	77. a	78. b	79. b	80. a
81. a	82. a	83. b	84. b	85. a	86. b	87. a	88. b	89. b	90. b
91. a	92. a	93. a	94. b	95. a	96. b	97. a	98. a	99. b	100. b
101. b	102. a	103. b	104. b	105. a	106. a	107. b	108. b	109. a	110. b
111. b	112. a	113. a	114. b	115. b	116. b	117. a	118. b	119. a	120. a
121. a	122. a	123. b	124. b	125. b	126. b	127. b	128. b	129. a	130. a
131. b	132. a	133. b	134. b	135. b	136. b	137. a	138. a	139. a	140. b
141. a	142. a	143. a	144. a	145. b	146. b	147. a	148. a	149. b	150. b
151. a	152. b	153. b	154. a	155. b	156. a	157. b	158. a	159. b	160. a
161. b	162. a	163. b	164. b	165. a	166. a	167. a	168. b	169. b	170. b
171. a	172. a								

www.ingramcontent.com/pod-product-compliance
Lightning Source LLC
Chambersburg PA
CBHW082051230426
43670CB00016B/2849